# THE MICROSCOPE
## BOOK

Shar Levine &
Leslie Johnstone

Illustrated by David Sovka

**Sterling Publishing Co., Inc.**
New York

To my son, Joshua, on the occasion of his bar mitzvah and, as always, my thanks to Paul, Shira, and Dorothy for their love and support. And to anyone who actually reads dedications, I have to tell you all that I work with the world's best co-author!

—S.L.

To Alison Hunter: Alison, this one's for you! My thanks to Mark, Christopher, Nicholas, and Megan for helping me find the time to work on this book.

—L.J.

To my love, Roseanne, and to my children, James and Rachel. And to my students and colleagues at Maimonides Secondary School in Vancouver, B.C. *Sumus quod sumus.*

—D.S.

The authors would like to thank the following people for their technical assistance and invaluable help: Sarah Hamblin for her help with the slides; Andrew Kay for being a great computer doctor; Dr. Elaine Humphrey and Dr. Ellen Rosenberg of the University of British Columbia; and Craig Siddall for being the big kahuna. Thanks also to Liz and Liz of Techno Kids, Vancouver, B.C.

**Library of Congress Cataloging-in-Publication Data**

Levine, Shar, 1953–
    The microscope book / Shar Levine, Leslie Johnstone;
illustrations by David Sovka.
        p.    cm.
    Includes index.
    Summary: An introduction to microscopes and magnification with
experiments using such easily obtained materials as comic books,
leaves, hair, and potatoes.
    ISBN 0-8069-4898-1
    1. Microscopes—Juvenile literature.    2. Microscopy—Juvenile
literature.    3. Microscopes—Experiments—Juvenile literature.
4. Microscopy—Experiments—Juvenile literature.    [1. Microscopes.
2. Microscopy—Experiments.    3. Experiments.]    I. Johnstone,
Leslie.    II. Sovka, David, ill.    III. Title.
QH278.L48    1996
502'.8'2—dc20                                                    95-43239
                                                                          CIP
                                                                          AC

Designed by Judy Morgan
Edited by Isabel Stein
Photomicrographs by the authors and Sarah Hamblin

3    5    7    9    10    8    6    4    2

First paperback edition published in 1996 by
Sterling Publishing Company, Inc.
387 Park Avenue South, New York, N.Y. 10016
© 1996 by Shar Levine and Leslie Johnstone
Distributed in Canada by Sterling Publishing
℅ Canadian Manda Group, One Atlantic Avenue, Suite 105
Toronto, Ontario, Canada M6K 3E7
Distributed in Great Britain and Europe by Cassell PLC
Wellington House, 125 Strand, London WC2R 0BB, England
Distributed in Australia by Capricorn Link (Australia) Pty Ltd.
P.O. Box 6651, Baulkham Hills, Business Centre, NSW 2153, Australia
*Printed in Hong Kong*
*All rights reserved*

Sterling ISBN 0-8069-4898-1 Trade
0-8069-4899-X Paper

# Contents

# Preface

Wouldn't you like to have super powers like your favorite superhero? You could see things far away. You could tell what something was made of! You could be gigantic compared to other living creatures. Your eyes would be so powerful that they could see the atoms that make up things in the world around you. Guess what? Using a microscope you, too, can have super powers. You are about to enter the exciting world of the microscope. By doing the simple experiments in this book, you can see tiny one-celled creatures living in water and watch yeast grow. You can make mushrooms "bloom" before your very eyes. Find out about the fossils in your toothpaste. You'll discover the uniqueness of fingerprints and fish scales. You can even create art on microscope slides! Best of all, you won't have to harm or kill any living thing to do all this. There's no need to rip the legs off insects or scrape the powder off butterfly wings in order to appreciate a microscope. You can learn just as much without destroying any life forms.

Microscopes may look complicated, but they aren't. Using these simple step-by-step instructions, you'll be an expert in no time. The experiments are ordered so you will learn many skills as you go along. While it is always tempting to jump ahead and try an experiment with a catchy title, if you do, you might miss an important technique that was used in an earlier experiment. If you're anxious to skip ahead, try reading through the book first, so that you understand the instructions and the methods used. If you don't understand a word, you can find it in the glossary at the back of the book. You and your parents don't have to know too much science to enjoy working with a microscope, and just about all the materials you'll need probably can be found around your house.

If you find that your slide looks different from the one shown in the book, don't fret. Try to make several slides and see if one more closely resembles the picture. We made all the slides using the same techniques we described in this book, but some of our slides may be clearer because we may have used a better microscope than you are using.

This book will no doubt make you want to learn more. Your library probably has many books on microscopes. Ask a librarian for help in finding them.

We have not used any special stains or other hard-to-find chemicals in this book. All the chemicals are available in grocery, stationery, or drug stores. Some books you read may recommend other chemicals or stains. Before you use any chemicals, make sure to get permission and help from an adult, as some chemicals are very poisonous. Keep a journal of the things you have seen under the microscope. Use this book to create a great science project. You can even bring some of your slides to school to share with your classmates. You are about to discover strange new worlds with your microscope. Remember—no matter how small you may be, you are still bigger than all the things you are about to view!

  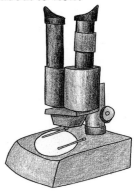

# A NOTE TO PARENTS AND TEACHERS

The microscopic world is fascinating to children of all ages; they are delighted to see so much life growing in a drop of water. Children will happily spend hours peering through a microscope. Look around your house or classroom; there are so many things that will make interesting slides. Ask children what they'd like to see close up.

We've tried to make the experiments as safe and as foolproof as possible. Closely following the instructions will ensure success. The experiments in the book are structured so that the first time a technique or concept is introduced it is described in detail. In subsequent chapters, there will be a reference to the experiment that explained the technique. Scientific words are printed in boldface type and defined the first time they are used; many also appear in the glossary at the back of the book. Unlike many microscopy books, ours does not contain experiments in which insects, frogs, or other living creatures are dissected or killed. *The Microscope Book* is intended to teach children basic techniques and observation skills without destroying any life forms. We do not recommend growing any bacterial cultures or using blood to make slides. These can be dangerous if not handled correctly.

If you do not own a microscope, don't despair. A magnifying glass can be used to perform some of the experiments in this book. Universities, colleges, and even some companies sell off their used microscopes. Call the purchasing department and ask if there are any microscopes for sale. Consult the yellow pages of the telephone book in your area for other sources of student level, inexpensive microscopes.

Encourage children to keep a journal of the things they see through the microscope. If you are a teacher, have the class write a report on the different kinds of microscopes that were developed through the ages, or have students bring in magazine photographs made with the electron microscope. You may even wish to create a wall of these photographs and ask the class to guess what the subject of each photograph is. Universities and colleges also may offer tours of their science and research facilities. You can organize a field trip to one so your class can see a powerful microscope in action. The most important thing is to have fun! Be prepared for squeals of delight as children peer through a microscope and discover a whole new world.

# SAFETY FIRST

Before you begin any of the activities in the book, there are a few do's and don'ts you need to follow so that you can use your microscope safely.

## Do's

**1.** Ask an adult before handling any materials, foods or equipment.
**2.** Have an adult handle all sharp objects such as knives or razor blades.
**3.** Wash your hands after performing the experiments.
**4.** Tie back long hair while you work, and avoid wearing clothing with long, loose sleeves, which could knock things over.
**5.** Keep your work area clean, and clean up any spills immediately.
**6.** Read all the steps of any experiment carefully and be sure you know what to do before you begin the experiment.
**7.** Always work in a well-ventilated area with adequate lighting.
**8.** Tell an adult immediately if you hurt yourself in any way.
**9.** Keep all supplies, tools, chemicals, and experiments out of the reach of very young children.

## Don'ts

**1.** If you are allergic or sensitive to any foods or other substances such as mould or dust, do not use them to perform experiments.
**2.** Do not taste, eat, or drink any of the experiments.
**3.** Do not kill, or be cruel to, any living creatures in your experiments.
**4.** Never look at the sun or another strong light source through your magnifying lens or microscope.

# LIST OF EQUIPMENT

Before you get started, have the following basic supplies and equipment handy. Read each experiment through before you start slicing and dicing the samples. Individual experiments require additional supplies that can, for the most part, be found in or around your home, or at a grocery store, drug store, stationery store, photography shop, or science store. Before you begin an experiment, gather together all the materials that you need to do it. Make sure that you have an adult's permission before using any sharp objects or handling any equipment. If you need extra slides or other scientific supplies, consult the yellow pages of your telephone directory under *Scientific instruments*, or check out specialty science and toy stores.

## You Will Need

- microscope
- slides
- cover slips (cover glasses)
- tweezers
- eyedropper
- tincture of iodine
- tissue paper
- India ink
- lens paper
- notebook
- pen and pencil
- colored pencils
- **stage micrometer** or clear plastic ruler
- compass or jar lid for drawing circles
- homemade microtome (see page 36 for instructions and supplies)
- razor knife or single-sided razor blade (to be used by an adult)
- stick-on paper notes (small size)
- magnifying glass
- petroleum jelly
- clear, colorless nail polish
- scissors

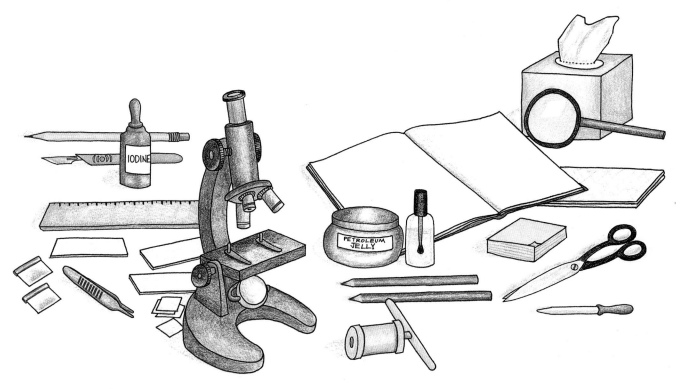

# Light, Lenses & Microscopes

*B*efore there were today's microscopes, there were magnifying glasses. And before that, there was just plain old water! To better understand how microscopes work, let's begin with the basics: how lenses bend light to magnify things.

# Bend and Stretch

*The first person to discover something about the bending of light probably was a prehistoric spear-fisher. Using a pointed stick to spear a fish, this person soon discovered that the fish seen in the water wasn't in a direct line with the spear. With a great deal of trial and error, the spear-fisher soon discovered that the spear must be pointed where the fish wasn't, in order to catch dinner. Try this experiment to show how light bends.*

## You Will Need

- a clear glass jar that holds 1 cup (240 mL)*
- ¼ cup (60 mL) water
- ¼ cup (60 mL) cooking oil
- ¼ cup (60 mL) rubbing alcohol
- plastic ruler

## What to Do

**1.** Pour the water into the jar.
**2.** Place the ruler in the jar so that it rests at an angle against the rim of the jar.
**3.** Carefully pour the cooking oil down the ruler onto the water. Do not mix. The oil should now be floating on the water.
**4.** Gently pour the rubbing alcohol down the ruler onto the oil layer. You should now have three layers.
**5.** Look at the ruler from different angles: above the jar, from the side of the jar, and directly in front of the jar.
**6.** When you are finished with your observations, pour the mixture down the sink. Do not drink or taste it.

**Bending of light in three liquids.**

*mL is the abbreviation for **millilitres**.*

## What Happened

The sections of the ruler appeared to be of different sizes in each liquid. The section that appeared the largest was in the oil. The section in the water appeared the next largest; the section in the rubbing alcohol was the least magnified. Since you know that the ruler actually could not have changed size, something must have happened to make it seem larger.

You were able to see the ruler because light was reflected from it. Light travels very quickly; in air or in a vacuum, about 186 000 miles (300 000 km) in one second. When light travels through different mediums (for example, glass, water, oil, and alcohol), it travels more slowly than it does through a vacuum or through air. Different substances slow light down by different amounts, depending on their **optical density**. When light passes from one medium to another at an angle, the change in the speed of the light at the boundary between the substances causes the light to bend. The bending of light is called **refraction.** The ratio of the speed of light in a vacuum to its speed in a particular substance is called the **index of refraction** of the substance. A substance with a large index of refraction causes the light to bend a great deal; a substance with a small index of refraction bends light less.

| THE INDEXES OF REFRACTION OF SOME COMMON SUBSTANCES | | |
| --- | --- | --- |
| Air: 1.0003 • Cottonseed oil: 1.47 | | |
| Water: 1.33 • Olive oil: 1.48 | | |
| Ethanol: 1.36 • Window glass: 1.51 | | |
| Glycerine: 1.46 • Diamond: 2.42 | | |

The larger the index of refraction, the more dense the medium is, and the more slowly light travels in that medium. The oil, which bent the light more than the water or alcohol in the experiment, has the largest index of refraction of all three liquids. A microscope uses the principles of refraction to focus light on samples and enlarge images as they travel through its curved glass lenses.

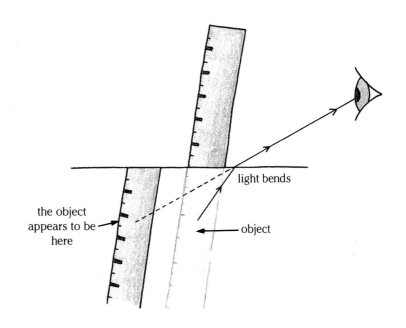

the object appears to be here

light bends

object

**Diagram of light rays, showing the refraction of light in the experiment.**

# A Drop of Water

People in ancient times knew that a drop of water that fell onto a grain of sand or onto a small insect made the object it fell on look larger than it actually was. A Roman philosopher named Seneca (4 B.C.– 65 A.D.) observed that "letters, though small and indistinct, are seen enlarged and more distinctly through a glass globe filled with water." The first person to explain this occurrence was Ptolemy, a Greek astronomer and mathematician who lived in the second century A.D. He said that the light was bent because it changed speed as it moved from one substance to another. Do this simple experiment to see how it works.

## You Will Need

- a page of print from a newspaper or magazine
- a sheet of clear plastic food wrap
- eyedropper
- a cup of water
- other clear, colorless liquids such as white corn syrup or glycerine

## What to Do

**1.** Spread out the page of print on a flat surface.
**2.** Cover it with the sheet of clear plastic film.
**3.** Look at the letters of the print through the plastic film.
**4.** With the eyedropper, place a drop of water over some of the letters.
**5.** Look at the letters through the water drop.
**6.** Repeat steps 4 and 5 using your other clear, colorless liquids.

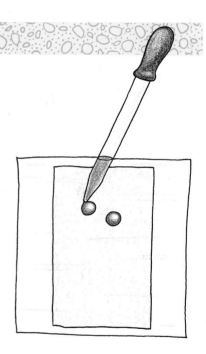

## What Happened

If you look at the liquids from the side, you will see that they form dome-shaped (convex) droplets, which are wider in the middle and thinner at the edges. Some lenses in a microscope also are convex. The letters looked larger when you looked at them through the water drops. The light in the room reflected off the page of print and travelled through the drop to your eyes. Water is denser than air, so at the boundary between the water and air, the light was bent, or refracted, which made the letters appear to be bigger than they looked without the drop. The syrup and glycerine drops also bent the light. Because these liquids are denser than either air or water, they slowed the light down more and bent it even more than the air and water did, which caused the letters seen through glycerine or syrup to appear even bigger than the letters you saw through the water drop.

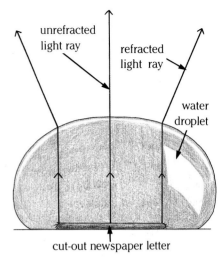

**The optics of a water drop.**

Sometimes when you shine light through a lens, you see a rainbow. In daily life, this may be beautiful, but rainbows are not desirable in microscope work, because they interfere with your view of what you are looking at. The rainbow effect is known as **chromatic aberration.** There are two ways of eliminating chromatic aberration. One is to coat microscope lenses with special materials; the other method is to use compound lenses (two or more lenses glued together) instead of single lenses.

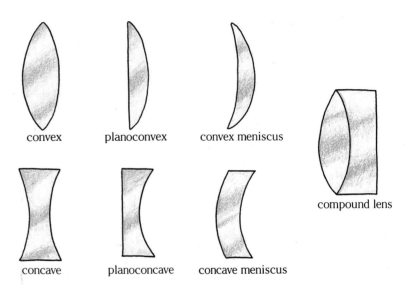

**The six basic types of lenses, and a compound lens.**

# Make a Spectacle of Yourself

You have convex lenses that you take with you everywhere you go: one in each eye. Behind the protective, transparent outer layer, called the cornea, light enters your eye through a small opening in the iris called the **pupil** (the small black space in the center of your eye), and then it is bent by the lens. The lens in your eye is held in place by small muscles, which cause it to flatten when you look at objects that are far away and bulge when you look at objects that are near. The bent light travels through a transparent, jellylike mass behind the lens until it is focused, upside down, on a light-sensitive layer at the back of your eye called the **retina**. The retina creates a signal that travels to your brain, allowing you to see. Your brain receives the upside-down signal and makes an adjustment so you see things right-side up.

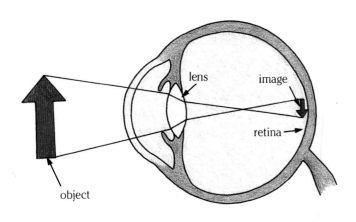

**How your eye sees an object.**

You may wear eyeglasses or know someone who wears eyeglasses. The lenses in prescription eyeglasses are known as "corrective lenses," because they correct the person's vision. If you have perfect vision, images are focused clearly on the retinas of your eyes. Some people wear eyeglasses because they are farsighted, which means that their uncorrected eyes focus images behind their retinas. Their eyeglasses have convex lenses that bend the light rays more than the lenses in the person's eyes do, so the rays will fall on their retinas. Nearsighted people have eyes that focus images in front of their retinas. Eyeglasses for nearsighted people have concave lenses, which bend light rays outward so they focus further back, on their retinas. Some people have astigmatism, which is caused by uneven or unsmooth corneas. Eyeglasses for people with astigmatism are specially curved to correct their vision. To see the effect of different kinds of lenses, try this simple experiment.

## You Will Need

- 3 pairs of glasses with different prescriptions (if possible one each from a person who is nearsighted, one who is farsighted, and who has astigmatism)
- this book

## What to Do

**1.** Place this book open to this page on a table.
**2.** Hold the eyeglasses, lens downwards, on top of the VISION words in the box.

**3.** Slowly lift the glasses off the page and watch the effect on the size of the print.
**4.** Repeat this with the other pairs of eyeglasses.
Note: do not wear another person's prescription eyewear as it may be harmful to your eyes and may cause eyestrain.

vision vision **vision**

## What Happened

If you had the eyeglasses of a far-sighted person, the print was magnified as you lifted the glasses. If you had the eyeglasses of a near-sighted person, the print seemed to shrink. If you had the eye-glasses of a person with astigma-tism, the type was distorted.

If you look closely at these eye-glasses, you will see that the lenses are curved differently and may vary in thickness. Lenses for people who need a stronger pre-scription (more correction to their vision) are usually thicker than those for people with a weaker prescription.

Should you wear your eyeglasses when you use the microscope? Here's an easy test to answer that question. Hold your eyeglasses at arm's length and look through them at the square. Rotate your lenses slowly while continuing to look at the square. If the square appears to become a rectangle when you rotate the lenses, you will need to wear your eyeglasses when you use the microscope. If the square doesn't appear to change shape, you can use the microscope without your eyeglasses.

# Cartwheels

*About a thousand years ago, the Arabian mathematician Alhazen (Abu Ali al-Hasan ibn al-Hasan ibn al-Haitham, 965-1038) was the first person to describe how a magnifying lens worked. He wrote a book called* The Treasury of Optics, *in which he analyzed and described vision and light. He observed that a convex piece of glass (a circular piece of glass that is thicker in the middle and thinner at the edge) could magnify the image of an object. Try this simple experiment, based on the writings of Alhazen, to see the effect a convex lens has on an image.*

## You Will Need

• a magnifying glass

• this book

## What to Do

**1.** Place this book, open to this page, on a table.

**2.** Place the magnifying glass over the drawing of a person.
**3.** Hold the magnifying glass at about arm's length away from your eye, and slowly lift the magnifying glass off the picture.
**4.** Keep lifting the magnifying glass until the image you are watching turns upside down.

## What Happened

As you first began to move the magnifying glass further away from the page, the image grew larger. At one point the image became fuzzy and then came back into focus upside down. This is because of the way the magnifying glass bends the light travelling to your eye from the page. When the magnifying glass is close to the page, you see what is known as a **virtual image.** This is an upright image that is larger than the image on the page. As you move the magnifying glass closer to your eye and away from the page, you see what is called a **real image,** which is upside down. Look at the diagrams to see how the light is bent by the lens to form the two types of images you saw.

Now that you know how lenses work, let's see how a microscope works.

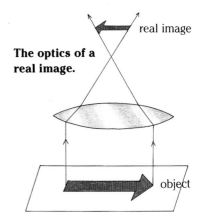

**The optics of a real image.**

real image

object

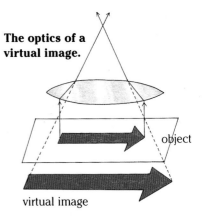

**The optics of a virtual image.**

object

virtual image

# The Compound Microscope

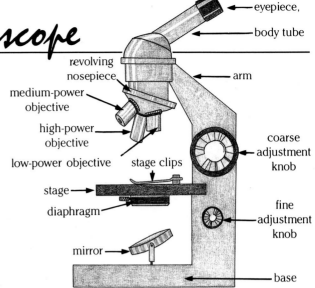

Many of you probably have magnifying glasses at home. You may be surprised to know that a magnifying glass actually is a simple microscope. Any microscope that has two or more lenses is called a **compound microscope.** Look around the house; perhaps you already have an old microscope that belonged to an older brother or sister, or maybe even to your parents or grandparents. It doesn't matter if a microscope is old, as long as it has all its parts and the lenses aren't scratched. More expensive microscopes tend to have better lenses and more features.

## You Will Need

- microscope
- paper stick-on notes or paper and cellophane tape
- pen or pencil

## What to Do

**1.** Compare your microscope to the illustrations at the right and find the one that looks most like yours.

**2.** Identify the different parts of the microscope. Copy the bold-faced words defined here onto paper notes and stick them onto the correct parts of your microscope. Once you know what everything is, you can begin exploring the microscopic world.

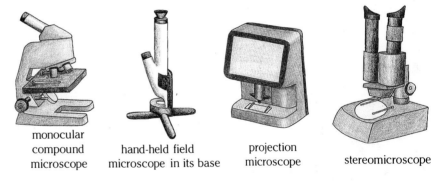

monocular compound microscope

hand-held field microscope in its base

projection microscope

stereomicroscope

**Several kinds of microscopes.**

### MAGNIFICATION

The markings on the objectives and eyepieces of your microscope tell you their magnifying **power,** how many times bigger they make the samples appear. To calculate the magnification of the things you are looking at, you need to multiply the power of the eyepiece by the power of the objective. If the eyepiece has the marking $10\times$ on it, it means that if it were used on its own, the objects you would see would appear to be 10 times bigger than they actually are. If you use the $10\times$ eyepiece with a low-power objective marked $4\times$, you will see objects that are magnified $10\times4 = 40$ times $(40\times)$. A $10\times$ objective with a $10\times$ eyepiece will make objects appear $10\times10 = 100$ times bigger. A $40\times$ objective with a $10\times$ eyepiece will magnify objects 400 times.

# MICROSCOPE PARTS AND THEIR USES

**A.** The **eyepiece** (ocular) is the part of the microscope closest to your eye, through which you look. It contains the ocular lens, which makes the image produced by the objective's lenses larger. Microscopes in which separate images are seen by both of the observer's eyes at the same time are called **binocular microscopes.** An eyepiece may be labelled with its magnification or power—for example 5× or 10× (meaning it enlarges 5 times or 10 times). Your microscope even may have a view screen or an attached projector that acts as an ocular lens.

**B.** The **body tube** holds the eyepiece in position over the revolving nosepiece and the objectives. The body tube may be straight up and down or slanted.

**C.** The **arm** is the curved metal piece that holds the body tube in place over the stage and the base.

**D.** The **revolving nosepiece** holds the objectives and allows you to change objectives while looking at a slide.

**E.** The **objectives** are the parts at the bottom of the body tube closest to the sample you are examining. Each objective has a lens and a tubelike holder, the mount. The longer mounts hold the stronger lenses (the high-power lenses). The shorter mounts hold the weaker lenses (the low-power lenses). Like the eyepieces, objectives come in various powers. Some microscopes have several objectives (for example 4×, 10×, 40×, and 100×; some microscopes only have one or two.

**F.** The **stage** is the flat surface on which you put your slides or samples.

**G.** The **stage clips** hold the slides in place on the stage. Some microscopes have a moveable stage, on which the slides are held in place by moveable jaws.

**H.** The **diaphragm** is used to adjust the amount of light shining through the sample on the stage. (Some microscopes do not have diaphragms.)

**I.** The **coarse adjustment knob** is the large knob used to adjust the position of the body tube, allowing you to quickly bring your sample into view.

**J.** The **fine adjustment knob** is the small knob used to change the position of the body tube by making small adjustments to the focus of your sample. Most microscopes have both coarse and fine adjustment knobs, but some have only one knob.

**K.** The **mirror** or **lamp,** located beneath the stage and diaphragm, increases the amount of light shining through your sample. The lamp may be battery-powered or it may plug into an electrical outlet.

**L.** Beneath the stage, some microscopes have a **condenser,** which collects and concentrates the light before it passes through the sample.

**M.** The **base** of the microscope is the heavy bottom part. It supports all the other parts of the microscope.

The earliest compound microscope is believed to have been invented by Hans and Zacharias Janssen, father and son lensmakers who lived in Holland around 1590. Working together, they made the first compound microscope, using a sliding tube and two lenses.

**The Janssen microscope.**

# Bringing It Into Focus

You're probably anxious to get started using your microscope. There are a few simple rules that you should follow to avoid damaging your microscope or your slides.

<table>
<tr><td colspan="2" align="center">FOCUSING</td></tr>
</table>

**1.** Remove the microscope from its box or cover. Always pick up your microscope correctly: grasp it firmly with two hands, one hand under the base and the other on the arm.

**2.** Place the microscope on a table, away from the edge. Move it to a position in which you can look comfortably through the eyepiece. You may want to sit on a chair or stool.

**3.** Make sure the low-power objective is in place over the hole in the stage. Use the coarse adjustment knob to raise the objective so its lowest end is about 1 inch (2.5 cm) above the stage.

**4.** Place your sample on the stage, and carefully secure it with the stage clips. Do not snap the stage clips, as you could damage them or the sample. Adjust the position of the sample so that it is over the hole in the stage.

**5.** Adjust the mirror or other light source to focus light through the sample. You should be able to see a circle of light when you look into the eyepiece. Never use your microscope in direct sunlight, as the reflected light could damage your eyes. If your microscope has a lamp, turn it on. You may need to replace the batteries or plug the lamp into an electrical outlet, depending on the style of microscope you have. When viewing very thick samples, you may have to shine light on the sample from above by using a table lamp or by placing your microscope in a brightly lit place.

**6.** Look at the objective from the side, and use the coarse adjustment knob to lower it until it is as close as possible to the sample.

**7.** Look through the eyepiece and use the coarse adjustment knob to focus upwards (moving away from the sample). This should bring the sample into view. If you go too far, simply begin again at step 6.

**8.** When the sample is in view, use the fine adjustment knob to bring it clearly into focus. If necessary, slide the sample gently sideways into the center of your **field of view.**

**9.** To use the high-power objective, turn the revolving nosepiece to bring it into position over your sample. You should be able to see the sample through the high-power objective, so you should only have to adjust the fine adjustment knob. Remember to always focus upwards so that the objective is moving away from the sample. Focusing downwards could break your slide or damage your lens.

**10.** Return to the low-power objective before removing the sample from the stage. To look at another sample, repeat steps 3 through 9.

**11.** When you are finished using the microscope, make sure the low-power objective is in position over the hole in the stage and turn off the light.

**12.** If your lenses get dirty, you may see spots or smudges when you look through the microscope, even if no sample is present. To clean them, always use lens paper, which you can purchase at a camera store. Tissue paper or cloth could damage your lenses. Breathe onto the surface of the lens and wipe in a circular motion.

**13.** Store your microscope, covered with a box or bag, in a safe, dry place, where it won't be knocked over. Use a plastic grocery bag, if necessary; label the bag or box; and remove the batteries when you store it, if your microscope has batteries. Make sure you support the box or bag when moving the microscope.

# COMIC STRIPS

Grab your favorite comic book or the colored comics pages from the weekend newspaper for the next experiment. Learn something new about microscopes and newspapers at the same time.

## You Will Need

- microscope
- comic book with colored pictures or the colored comics pages of the newspaper
- reading lamp and scissors
- paper and pen or pencil

## What to Do

**1.** Find a picture in the comics that is orange, green, flesh-colored, or purple; make sure it is large enough to cover the hole in your microscope stage.

**2.** Cut a 1 inch × 3 inch (2.5 cm × 7.5 cm) strip of paper with the picture you have chosen in the center of it.

**3.** Place the strip on the microscope stage and secure it with the stage clips.

**4.** Shine light onto the top of the paper, using the reading lamp.

**5.** Bring the sample into focus with the low-power objective, following steps given before on focusing.

**6.** Count the number of dots of one of the colors that you can see and record this number.

**7.** Change to the high-power objective and count the number of dots you see of the same color. Compare this number to the number you recorded under low power.

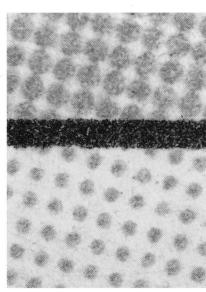

**Photomicrograph of colored comics under medium power (photographed at 120× and enlarged).**

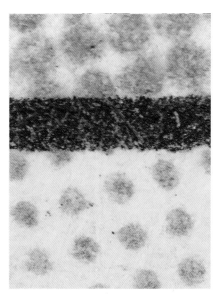

**Photomicrograph of colored comics under high power (photographed at 250× and enlarged).**

## What Happened

There were different-colored dots that made up the seemingly solid-colored pictures in the comics. Newspaper pictures are made with about 60 dots per linear inch (24 dots per cm). Printed pictures in magazines and books are made with as many as 400 dots per inch (160 dots per cm). Your brain blends the different dots together to form the colors you see.

You may have noticed that you could see more dots through the low-power objective than through the high-power objective. The area that you see through the microscope is called the **field of view.** When you switch from the low-power to the high-power objective, the objects appear to be larger, but you see fewer of them. To better understand this, you could compare the field of view to a dinnerplate. Under the low-power objective the dots are small, like marbles. Under the high-power objective, they appear to be large, like bowling balls. How many marbles do you think you could place on a dinnerplate? How many bowling balls? Try it and see!

---

### CONNECT THE DOTS

If you look closely at a newspaper picture, you probably can see that it is made up of dots. You may not be able to see the dots that make up pictures in magazines, because your eye can only see things that are larger than about one-tenth of a **millimetre** (0.1 mm). When the dots are smaller and closer together, your eye cannot distinguish between them and they appear as a solid color. This ability of your eyes to tell the dots apart is called their **resolving power.** When you magnify objects, you increase your resolving power. Unfortunately, light microscopes have a limit to their resolving power. At the highest power, light microscopes enable you to see objects about one-half micrometre (0.5 μm) in size. (A micrometre is .000001 metre). To see things smaller than this, you need an electron microscope.

# How Big Is It?

When you view a sample under the microscope, it may be difficult to judge what size it is. What was just a tiny speck now takes up the entire field of view. A **stage micrometer** is a slide equipped with a measuring scale, which allows you to measure very small objects. If your microscope came equipped with a stage micrometer, you can follow the directions below to use it. The best stage micrometers have lines that are very clear under the high-power objective; they can be quite expensive because they are difficult to make. If you don't have a stage micrometer, you still can make rough measurements using your microscope.

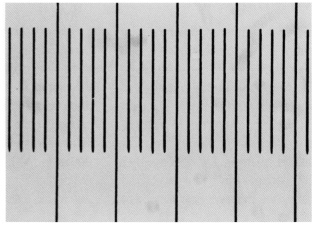

**Stage micrometer (magnified). Lines are 0.01 mm apart.**

## UNITS OF MEASUREMENT

Microscopists look at objects that are very, very tiny. Like other scientists, they use a system of measurement known as the International System of Units, or SI, based on the metric system. The metric system uses multiples of 10 and is based on a standard length of 1 metre. Microscopic objects are usually measured in either millimetres (mm) or micrometres (μm). A millimetre is 1/1000 of a metre. A micrometre is 1/1000 of a millimetre. Some metric units that we will need are given here, as well as some conversions from the common units used in the United States and Great Britain to metric units.

**Metric Units**

1 metre (m) = 100 centimetres (cm)

1 metre = 1000 millimetres (mm)

1 metre = 1 000 000 micrometres (μm)

1 centimetre = 10 millimetres (mm)

1 centimetre = 10 000 micrometres (μm)

1 millimetre = 1000 micrometres (μm)

1 litre (L) = 1000 millilitres (mL)

**From Common to Metric Units**

1 yard = 0.91 metre (m)

1 foot = 30.48 centimetres (cm)

1 inch = 2.54 centimetres (cm)

1 cup = .24 litre (L)

1 fluid ounce = 30 millilitres (mL)

1 teaspoon = 5 millilitres (mL)

1 tablespoon = 15 millilitres (mL)

**A ruler with inch and centimetre markings.**

## You Will Need

- microscope
- stage micrometer (slide with micrometre scale) or clear plastic metric ruler
- paper and pen or pencil

## What to Do

**1.** Place the stage micrometer or clear plastic ruler on the stage of your microscope and secure it with the stage clips.

**2.** Look at the stage micrometer or ruler under the low-power objective. Move the stage micrometer or ruler so that it lies across the widest part (the **diameter**) of the field of view. Count the number of millimetre divisions you can see. Write this number down. Use this number when measuring samples viewed under the low-power objective.

**3.** Look at the stage micrometer or ruler under a high-power objective, and count the number of millimetres across the diameter of the field of view. Write down this number also. This is the number you will use when measuring a sample viewed under the high-power objective.

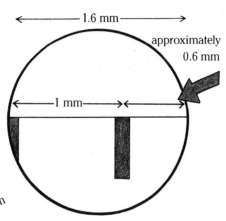

Calculating the size of the field of view using a stage micrometer under high power. (In this case it is 1.6 mm.)

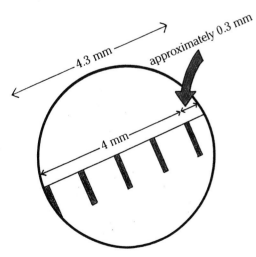

**Calculating the size of the field of view using a stage micrometer under low power. (In this case it is 4.3 mm.)**

**4.** Place the sample slide that you wish to measure on the stage of your microscope and secure it with the stage clips. First look at the sample with the low-power objective. Move the sample so that it stretches across the center of the field of view. How much of the field of view does the sample stretch across? For example, if the number of millimetre divisions you could see when you measured the field of view using your low-power objective was 20 and your sample stretches across half the field of view, then it stretches across 10 millimetres (10 mm). If the sample was smaller and covered roughly one-fourth of the field of view, then it covers 5 mm.

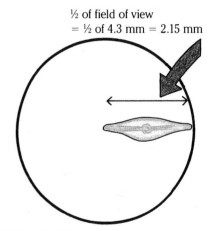

**Estimating the size of a sample based on the size of the field of view.**

**5.** If your sample stretches across only a very small portion of the field of view, try looking at it with the high-power objective. Make your calculations based on the width of your field of view under high power, which you measured earlier (step 3).

**6.** If your microscope has a **micrometer eyepiece**, an eyepiece with a built-in scale, you can use it to measure samples. (The scales, or **graticules**, also are sold separately.) You still will need the stage micrometer to calculate the size of the markings on the micrometer eyepiece, which will have different values with high- and low-power objectives.

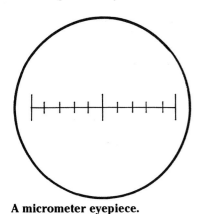

**A micrometer eyepiece.**

## FIELD OF VIEW DIAMETER UNDER HIGH POWER

If you know the diameter of the field of view under low power, you can calculate the diameter of the field of view for the medium- or high-power lenses of your microscope. For any one microscope, the field diameter multiplied by the total magnification of the microscope always gives you the same number; it is a constant:

field diameter · eyepiece magnification · objective magnification = constant
so if under low power the field of view diameter = 5 mm
and the objective is $10\times$ and the eyepiece is $4\times$
the constant is $5 \cdot 4 \cdot 10 = 200$

to calculate the field diameter ( y) under high power:
if the eyepiece is $10\times$ and the objective is $20\times$
the field diameter $y = 200/ (10 \cdot 20) = 200/200 = 1$
therefore y = 1 mm

# KEEPING A JOURNAL

Scientists keep records of their experiments so that they know what they have done and what happened when they did it. We know so much about the work of early scientists because of the detailed records they left in their journals. One of the earliest microscopists (1632–1723) was Anton van Leeuwenhoek (pronounced *Lay ven hook*), a Dutch merchant who ground lenses as a hobby. He became very expert at grinding lenses from high-quality glass and even from diamonds. The microscopes he designed and built were simple ones, but his lenses were of such high quality that he could

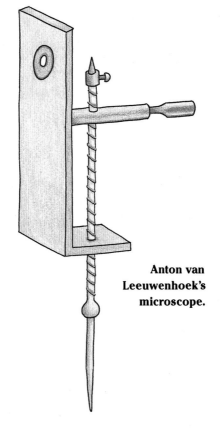

**Anton van Leeuwenhoek's microscope.**

see clear images of objects magnified 200 times, including tiny single-celled bacteria, which he called "beasties." He kept very detailed journals with drawings and descriptions of what he saw.

When you look at samples with your microscope, keep a record of your work in a notebook or on large index cards. You can create your own journal log or you can photocopy the blank form given here. Remember to label and store your slides in a safe place. If you are not making permanent slides, wash and dry the slides thoroughly after you are finished using them, and put them back in a box. Do not leave slides or cover glasses on the floor or on a table, as they may break and hurt others.

| DATE SAMPLE GATHERED: | DATE OF SLIDE: |
| --- | --- |
| WHAT SAMPLE IS: | WHERE SAMPLE IS FROM: |

HOW SAMPLE WAS PREPARED
METHOD:
STAINS:
MOUNT:

OBJECTIVE/EYEPIECE USED:

LIGHTING USED:

OBSERVATIONS:

ESTIMATED SIZE OF SAMPLE:

DRAWING OF SAMPLE:

## You Will Need

- microscope
- prepared slide
- unlined white paper
- a well-sharpened pencil
- a compass or jar lid about 4 inches (10 cm) in diameter
- colored pencils
- a ruler

## What to Do

**1.** Place the slide on the stage of your microscope and focus on your sample.

**2.** Use a pencil and compass or jar lid to draw a circle about 4 inches (10 cm) in diameter on the paper; it will represent your field of view.

**3.** Look through the eyepiece with one eye and look at the paper with the other eye. It may take you a while to be comfortable doing this.

**4.** Draw what you see through the eyepiece, as clearly as possible. Your drawings will be more realistic if you draw them in the colors you see.

**5.** Label the drawing. Include the magnification you are using. You may wish to include the sizes of any objects you have measured, using the steps in the How Big Is It? experiment, or estimated from the size of the field of view. Paste or tape your drawing onto your journal page or index card.

# Give Me an e

*If you think you know what the letter e looks like, think again. You'll be very surprised to discover the changes that lenses can make to the printed letter.*

## You Will Need

- a page of newspaper
- ruler and microscope

## What to Do

**1.** Find a section of print on the newspaper that contains a small letter e. Tear out a 2 inch × 3 inch (5 cm × 7.5 cm) piece of newspaper.

**2.** Make sure your microscope is in a brightly lit area, or use a table lamp to shine light onto the top of the newspaper.

**3.** Place the strip of paper on the stage of your microscope. Move it so that the letter e is in position under the low-power objective and secure it with the stage clips.

**4.** Carefully focus the microscope so that you can clearly see the letter e. Compare the e you see with your naked eye to the e you see with the microscope.

**5.** Look through the eyepiece while moving the paper in different directions—back and forth, side to side. Notice which way the magnified image moves.

**6.** Try the experiment with the letters a, f, h, and r.

**7.** Move the newspaper so that its torn edge is directly under the low-power objective lens. Refocus the microscope if necessary. Look at the fibres that make up the paper.

**Photomicrograph of the letter e (photographed at 250× and enlarged).**

**Photomicrograph of the edge of a torn paper (photographed at 250× and enlarged).**

## What Happened

When you looked at them through the microscope, the letters were bigger, but they also were upside down. Another strange thing: not only was the image upside down and backwards, but its movement also was backwards. When you moved the paper to the right, the image in the microscope moved to the left. When you moved the paper towards you, the image in the microscope moved away from you. The lenses inside the microscope bend the light so that the image you see is the reverse of the object you are looking at. When you focused on the edges of the paper, you could see the wood fibres from which the paper was made. The fibres even faced the same direction. This is called the grain of the paper; it is what holds the paper together.

# Sew Long

Have you ever tried to take a picture of someone standing in front of a distant mountain, lake, or other background? You may have found that either the person is in focus or the background is in focus, but not both. This is because your camera is unable to get both images to be in sharp focus at the same time. The same thing happens with your microscope. You probably have noticed that not everything you can see is in focus (or sharp) at the same time when you look through the microscope. As you focus on one area, another area seems to become fuzzy or unclear. This problem only gets worse when you go to a more powerful magnification. Here's an experiment to show you what happens.

**Hoary marmot, photographed in Yoho National Park, Canadian Rocky Mountains.**

## You Will Need

• Three ½-inch-long (1 cm) pieces of sewing thread, each a different color

• slide and cover slip

• clear nail polish or water

• tweezers

• microscope

## What to Do

**1.** Put the slide on a table and place a drop of colorless nail polish in the center of the slide. (This will create a permanent slide. If you haven't any nail polish, you can use water to make a temporary slide.)

**2.** Before the polish dries, use the tweezers to put a piece of sewing thread into the center of the nail polish so that the thread is parallel to the long side of the slide.

**3.** Use the tweezers to place a second piece of sewing thread of a different color across the top of the first piece of thread at right angles to form an X shape.

**4.** Carefully place a piece of thread of a third color across the top of the first two pieces of thread, at an angle to the others, so that the bottom pieces of thread still can be seen.

**5.** Hold the cover slip upright so that one edge of the slip touches the edge of the drop of nail polish or water.

**6.** Gently lower the cover slip over the three pieces of thread, trying not to trap any air bubbles under it.

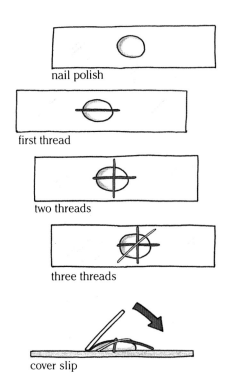

nail polish

first thread

two threads

three threads

cover slip

**Placing threads and cover slip on the slide.**

**7.** Look at your slide under the microscope, using the low-power objective. Center the point at which the three threads cross in your field of view. Focus on each of the three threads in turn. Repeat this using the high-power objective. Again focus on each of the three threads.

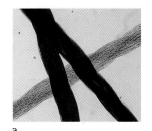

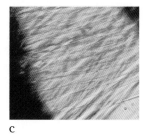

a                b                c

**Photomicrograph of the three threads, photographed under (a) low power (40 ×); (b) medium power (100 ×); (c) high power (400 ×); all enlarged.**

## What Happened

When you looked at your slide using the low-power objective, you probably were able to see all three threads pretty clearly. You might have had to use the fine adjustment knob a little bit to make each one a bit clearer. When you switched to the high-power objective, it became more difficult to focus on more than one of the threads at a time, because of the decrease in the **depth of field** as you went from the low-power objective to the high-power objective. The high-power objective bends the light more, so it has a narrower range of focus (depth of field) than the low-power objective does. When you are preparing samples for higher magnifications, you must ensure that they are very thin, so that all areas of the sample can be in focus at the same time.

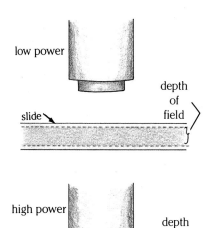

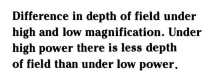

**Difference in depth of field under high and low magnification. Under high power there is less depth of field than under low power.**

Now that you know the basics of how a microscope works, it's time to get into the *real* experiments. If you come across a word you don't know or something you don't know how to do, check the index or glossary at the back of the book.

Some microscopes have a special type of lens called an **oil immersion lens**. This lens is used by placing a drop of oil on the top of the cover slip and adjusting the position of the front lens of the objective so that it is touching the oil drop. The oil bends the light more than the air would, so more light can enter the microscope. Oil immersion lenses make it easier to see samples, because they increase the amount of light going through the sample and the microscope and into your eye.

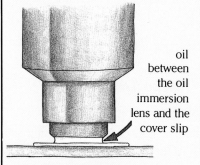

oil between the oil immersion lens and the cover slip

**An oil immersion lens.**

# Biology

Biology is the study of living things. From the early scientists like Anton van Leeuwenhoek and Robert Hooke, who looked at cells, to the genetic engineers of today, **microscopists** have played a major part in how scientists understand living things. Biologists use microscopes to study plants and animals. With this knowledge, they can create special plants that use less water to grow or will not be eaten by bugs. Biologists can even predict what physical characteristics parents will pass on to their children.

There are many areas of study within biology; for example, marine biology is the study of life in the ocean, botany is the study of plants, and genetics is the study of how certain traits are passed on from parents to their offspring.

Many people are excited about something new called **biotechnology**, an applied biological science that changes the characteristics of living things to serve a technological purpose. In 1984, a biotechnology company in the United States created OncoMouse, the first animal ever to be created and patented.

**Microbiology** is a special area of science that studies tiny living things (microorganisms). Louis Pasteur, who first identified yeast as a microorganism and developed a vaccine for rabies, was a microbiologist.

Using microscopes, scientists have been able to identify bacteria and viruses that cause disease. With this information, doctors can then begin to diagnose, prevent, or cure many of the world's diseases. Had it not been for the microscope, the causes of malaria, yellow fever, tuberculosis, cholera, rabies, and many other illnesses would not have been discovered. Today, powerful microscopes are used to examine many viruses, including the HIV virus that causes AIDS, in the hopes of finding a cure.

# Put a Cork in It

A thin slice of the cork from a wine bottle is a great thing to view under a microscope. Cork is made from the outer bark of a special kind of evergreen oak tree that grows in the Mediterranean area. Sheets of cork are carefully peeled off the tree, seasoned, and then finally boiled. Using your microscope, you can study the pores containing pockets of air, called **lenticels**, which the cork contains and see which way the lenticels are pointing.

One of the most famous pictures of cork as viewed through a microscope was drawn by an English scientist, Robert Hooke (1635–1703). Hooke used an early compound microscope made for him by an expert instrument maker.

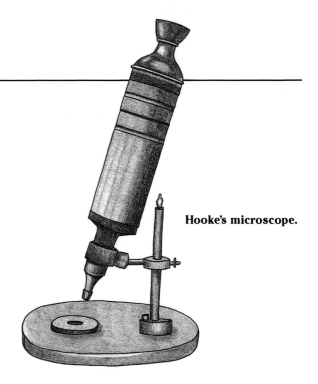

Hooke's microscope.

## You Will Need

- a cork from a bottle
- sharp razor knife or single-sided razor blade
- an eyedropper
- water
- slide and cover slip
- tweezers
- tissue paper or paper towel
- microscope
- an adult helper
- petroleum jelly

## What to Do

**1.** Have an adult cut several thin slices of cork, using the razor knife or razor blade. The thinner the slice, the easier it will be to see the cork under the microscope.
**2.** Follow the steps in the box for making a wet mount of the cork.
**3.** Observe your slide under the microscope using the low-power objective.

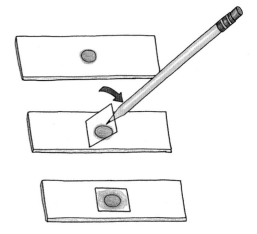

**Cover slip is lowered into position over a water drop containing a sample. Top: the drop. Middle: lowering the cover slip. Bottom: the finished wet mount.**

**Photomicrograph of a cork section in wet mount (photographed at 100× and enlarged).**

## What Happened

The magnified cork has air pockets surrounded by thin walls. Hooke wrote that the individual pockets looked like little rooms. He called them **cells** (from the Latin word cellula, meaning a small room), because they reminded him of cells in a monastery or prison. We still use the word *cell* today. In cork, the cells look like small rectangular boxes. The cells are empty because all the living matter has died, leaving behind air pockets. These pockets or lenticels are formed in only one direction. The trapped air in these spaces causes the cork to float. Corks are cut at an angle to keep the wine from leaking through. In addition to its use as a stopper for bottles, cork is used for many other things, including life preservers, insoles, and even floor tiles.

*Amaze your parents and teachers with this bit of science trivia: The first person to use cork as a stopper for wine bottles was a French monk, Dom Pierre Pérignon.*

DOM PERIGNON

# Onion Rings

As strange as this may sound to you, the onion in your refrigerator or cupboard is a living thing. By examining a slice of onion under a microscope, you will see the specialized plant cells contained in its see-through lining. Don't worry about crying when you peel the onion to prepare the sample, you can use your tears as part of another experiment!

## You Will Need

- raw cooking onion
- knife and tweezers
- eyedropper and water
- slide and cover slip
- tissue or paper towel
- microscope
- tincture of iodine, available in most drugstores*

## What to Do

**1.** Slice the raw onion and cut one of the onion rings into ¼-inch (6 mm) sections.

**2.** Remove the thin skin from the inner, concave side of the onion section by pulling it gently with tweezers.

**3.** Make a wet mount of the onion skin, flattening the onion skin in the drop of water.

**4.** Examine your slide under the microscope, using both the low-power and high-power objectives.

**5.** Remove your slide from the microscope and place it on a piece of tissue or paper towel.

**6.** Stain the sample with tincture of iodine by pulling the stain, following the directions in the box.

**7.** Examine your slide again under both the low-power and high-power objectives. Compare these images with the way the onion skin looked without the iodine stain.

**8.** Remove and wash the slide and cover slip with soap and water immediately after you have finished.

**9.** If working with the onion brought tears to your eyes, don't wipe your face with a tissue. Lean over a clean slide and collect several tears in the center of the slide. Put this slide in a warm dry place to dry out for the experiment called Crystal Gazing.

*Warning: tincture of iodine will stain skin and clothing and will sting if you get it in a cut. It will damage the metal parts of your microscope. Make sure you wipe up any spilled droplets immediately!*

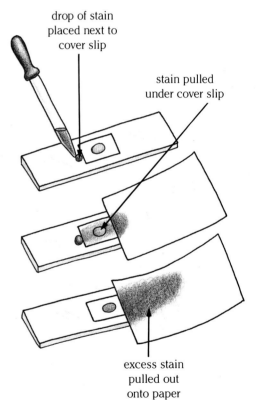

drop of stain placed next to cover slip

stain pulled under cover slip

excess stain pulled out onto paper

**Steps in pulling a stain. Top: drop of stain is placed next to cover slip. Middle: The stain is pulled under the cover slip. Bottom: The excess stain is pulled out onto the paper towel.**

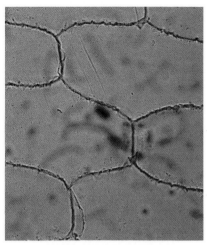

Photomicrograph of unstained onion skin (photographed at 400× and enlarged).

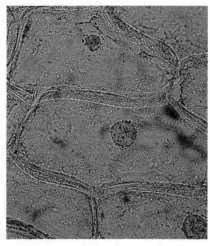

Photomicrograph of stained onion skin (photographed at 400× and enlarged).

## PULLING A STAIN

**A.** Use an eyedropper to place a drop of stain next to the cover slip.

**B.** Carefully touch a dry piece of tissue or paper towel to the side of the cover slip opposite the drop of stain.

**C.** The drop will move through the sample, and the tissue or towel will become damp.

**D.** Add more stain, until the stain begins to show on the tissue or paper towel. Carefully blot up any extra stain from the sides of the cover slip.

## What Happened

Using the microscope, you saw rows of long, box-shaped structures. These are the cells of the onion skin. They resemble the cells you saw in the cork experiment, but they are different, because they are still alive. You may have seen a little blob that looked like a bubble inside one or more cells. This is called the cell **nucleus**; it directs the cell's activities. Staining the cells with the tincture of iodine made it easier to see the cells and their parts. Most parts of the cell turn yellow, and the nucleus becomes yellowish brown. You probably also could see the **cell walls**, which are the nonliving supports of the cell, and the **cytoplasm**, the fluid inside the cell. You may also see **vacuoles**, areas that store waste materials and water in the cell. Onion skin cells are used by the onion for protection. Compare your onion skin cells to the ones in the photograph.

*Why do people cry when they cut onions? Onions contain oils that irritate the eyes. The tear glands in the eyes produce tears to flush out these irritating oils.*

# Greensleeves

If you tried to describe plants to a visitor from another planet, what would you say? You would probably say, among other things, that plants are green. Plants are green for an important reason. They contain a pigment called **chlorophyll**, which plants use to produce their own food. This process is called **photosynthesis**. You probably think that most plants live on the land. In fact, there are also many plants living in water. Here is a way to look at one of these plants.

## You Will Need

- *Elodea* (an aquatic plant available at aquariums and pet stores)
- tweezers and scissors
- slide and cover slip
- eyedropper
- microscope

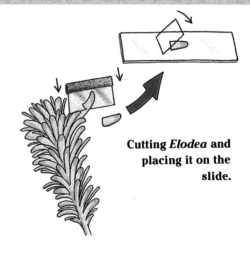

**Cutting *Elodea* and placing it on the slide.**

## What to Do

**1.** Cut a leaf from the stalk of the *Elodea* plant.
**2.** Make a wet mount of the leaf (see pg. 29), using some water that came in the plant's plastic bag. Use tweezers to flatten the leaf slightly. Be careful not to squash the leaf.
**3.** Examine your slide under the microscope, using both the low-power and high-power objectives.

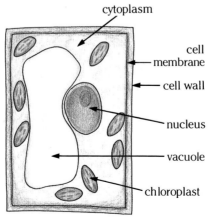

cytoplasm

cell membrane

cell wall

nucleus

vacuole

chloroplast

**Diagram of *Elodea* as seen through the microscope.**

## What Happened

You saw large, rectangular cells, which have cell walls, cytoplasm, and nuclei. You also saw small green dots in the cells, **chloroplasts**, the parts of plant cells that contain chlorophyll. The chloroplasts look as though they are swimming in the cytoplasm, but in fact it is the cytoplasm that is moving around. The chloroplasts are simply being carried along by this **cytoplasmic streaming** or movement. Chloroplasts are found in cells that produce food for the plant, such as leaf cells.

# Plant Pipelines

*Do you enjoy using a straw to slurp up a cold drink from a glass? Plants also have a way of drinking up liquids. Here are two ways of examining how liquids move through plants.*

## You Will Need

- glass jar or container
- water
- red food coloring or red ink
- stalk of celery
- sharp knife
- adult helper
- slides and cover slips
- tweezers and eyedropper
- paper towels
- microscope

## What to Do

**1.** Fill a glass halfway with water and add 8 to 10 drops of red food coloring or ink.

**2.** Have an adult trim the root end from the celery stalk. Do not cut off the leaves.

**3.** Immediately place the cut end of the celery in the water; let it stand overnight.

**4.** The next day, remove the stalk from the water and dry it with a paper towel.

**5.** Have an adult cut off about 2 inches (5 cm) of celery from the bottom of the stalk and then cut a few very thin slices across the stalk.

**6.** Make wet mounts of the celery slices (see page 29).

**7.** Examine your slide under both the low-power and high-power objectives.

**8.** Strip off a red string of celery by pulling it lengthwise from the remaining stalk. Have an adult cut a 1½-inch (1-cm) section of the string. Make a wet mount of the piece of celery string.

**9.** Examine your slide under the low-power objective of your microscope.

**The celery experiment. (1) Dyeing the celery. (2) Cutting a 2-inch (5cm) piece. (3) Cutting a strip of celery string.**

## What Happened

The leaves of the celery turned red. The stalk was red in stripes because the red dye colored the strings of the celery. The sections of the celery have red dots along their outside edges. These dots are the **xylem** cells of the celery stem. Xylem cells are the cells that transport water and nutrients in plants and provide support. The dye shows you where the water went inside the stalk. In the strip of the celery string, the xylem cells look like long rectangular boxes; they make up a tube, very much like the straws you drink through. In plants, water comes into the stalk from the roots, which absorb it from the soil.

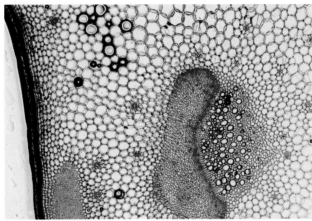

Photomicrograph of cross-section of a celery stalk; photographed at 40× and enlarged.

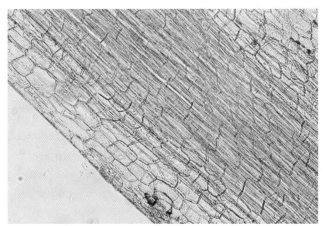

Photomicrograph of string cells; photographed at 100× and enlarged.

# Fresh-Cut Flowers

*There's more than one way to appreciate flowers. You can smell them. You can look at them. You can take them apart and see the exciting structures inside of them. In this experiment you will make a special piece of equipment called a **microtome**, which will help you make thin sections of samples and will probably prevent your getting cuts from a sharp knife.*

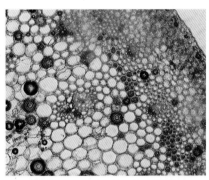

**Photomicrograph of a gladiolus stem in cross-section; photographed at 100 × and enlarged.**

**Photomicrograph of a leaf in cross-section; photographed at 400 × and enlarged.**

## You Will Need

- empty thread spool with a hole ³⁄₁₆ inch (5 mm) in diameter
- metal nut and bolt about ³⁄₁₆ inch (5 mm) in diameter
- ice cream stick
- waterproof glue that will stick to metal and wood
- fine-point waterproof marking pen
- flower stem (soft stems like those of tulips and daffodils work best)
- carrot and flower leaf
- razor knife or single-edged razor blade
- small bowl and water
- tweezers and microscope
- slide and cover slip
- adult helper

## What to Do

**1.** Make a microtome (see box).
**2.** Cut a 1-inch (2.5 cm) section of flower stem and insert its end into the microtome.
**3.** Have an adult cut several thin sections of the stem, using the razor blade or knife. Prepare a wet mount of the stem (see page 29).
**4.** Examine your slide under low and high power. Set it aside.
**5.** Cut a long thin strip from the center of the leaf. Place the strip between two strips of carrot cut to fit in the microtome. Insert both the leaf and the carrot pieces in the microtome.
**6.** Have an adult cut several sections of the leaf using the razor blade or knife. Prepare a wet mount of the leaf.
**7.** Examine your leaf slide under low power and high power.

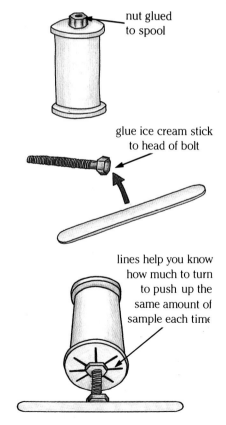

nut glued to spool

glue ice cream stick to head of bolt

lines help you know how much to turn to push up the same amount of sample each time

**Steps in microtome construction.**

## MAKING A MICROTOME

**A.** Thread the metal bolt through the empty thread spool and screw on the nut. Carefully remove the bolt and have an adult attach the nut to the spool using waterproof glue. Allow the glue to set.

**B.** Have an adult glue the head of the bolt to the middle of the flat side of an ice cream stick. Allow the glue to set. The ice cream stick acts as your handle.

**C.** Screw the metal nut and spool onto the bolt. Do not tighten the bolt; thread it on, leaving a space at the top for your sample.

**D.** Use a fine-point waterproof marking pen to draw eight equally spaced lines around the flat bottom surface of the spool (see drawing). These markings help you know how far to turn the stick so you can make each section you cut the same thickness. You are now ready to use your microtome.

**E.** Have an adult cut your sample to fit inside the hole in the spool with nothing sticking out. A piece of carrot can be used to fill in any empty spaces or to support oddly shaped samples. Turn the handle of your microtome to raise the carrot and sample a bit.

**F.** Have an adult slice across the top of your sample with a razor knife or single-edged razor blade. Dip the blade and the section into a bowl of water. The section should float off the blade. Turn the handle and cut another section. Repeat the dipping and cutting until you have several sections.

**G.** Use tweezers to transfer your sections to slides. Make wet mounts (see page 29).

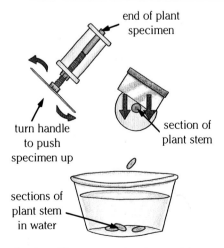

**Cutting flower stem sections with a microtome.**

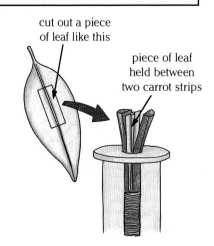

**A leaf is placed between carrot pieces in the microtome for slicing.**

## What Happened

The sections of stem that you cut are made up of several different types of cells. The outer layer, or **epidermis**, surrounding the stem is made up of thin cells that protect the stem. There are bundles of cells packed closely together, called **vascular bundles**. Vascular bundles are made up of **xylem** cells, which carry water within the stem, and of **phloem** cells, which carry nutrients. Xylem and phloem are arranged differently in different types of flowers. In flowers that grow from bulbs, like tulips, the bundles are scattered throughout the stem. In the stems of other flowers, like roses and geraniums, the xylem and phloem cells are arranged in neat circles.

The leaf section also is made up of different types of cells. On the top and bottom of the leaf there are the thin **epidermis** cells. You may see small openings (**stoma**) in the bottom epidermis, surrounded by slightly fatter cells, **guard cells**; to learn more about them see Leaf Me Alone. Just under the epidermis on the upper side of the leaf are some tall, oblong cells called **palisade cells**, which make food for the plant. Then there are many roundish spongy cells, which make up the bulk of the leaf. Inside the spongy cells are some bundles of xylem and phloem cells, which appear darker.

# Leaf Me Alone

*Have you ever wondered what a leaf looks inside? It looks like miniature towns with tiny roads linking them. Maybe you think you'd need a vivid imagination to see this, but after this next experiment, you will be able to choose your own words to describe this wondrous sight.*

TRANSPORT SYSTEM AT WORK.

## You Will Need

- a leaf from a geranium plant
- tweezers
- slide and cover slip
- eyedropper and water
- India ink or tincture of iodine*
- microscope
- paper towel

## What to Do

**1.** Roll the leaf back and forth between your palms in order to loosen the top layer.

**2.** Use the tweezers to separate the top layer from the bottom layer of the leaf. Some people find it easier to peel the top away, while others find it easier to peel the bottom.

**3.** Rip off a tiny piece of the bottom layer of the leaf and place it so the underside of the leaf faces upwards on the center of a clean slide.

**4.** Make a wet mount of the sample, following the directions on page 29.

**5.** Observe your slide under the microscope, using the low- and high-power objectives.

**6.** Stain your sample using a drop of iodine or India ink. (See the directions for pulling a stain, page 31). Observe it again using low and high power. What difference does this make to what you see?

*\*Warning: tincture of iodine will stain skin and clothing and will sting if you get it in a cut. It will damage the metal parts of your microscope, so be sure to wipe up any spilled droplets immediately.*

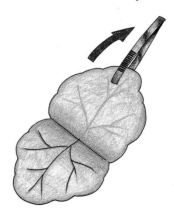

**Layers being peeled from a leaf.**

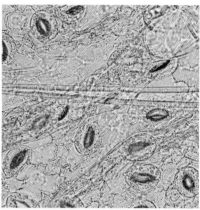

**Photomicrograph of geranium leaf epidermis without stain; photographed at 100 × and enlarged.**

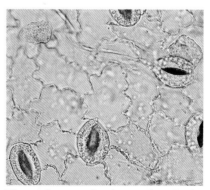

**Photomicrograph of geranium leaf epidermis with iodine stain; photographed at 400 × and enlarged.**

## What Happened

The layer of skin on the outside of the leaf is called the **epidermis**. It has interlocking cells, which fit together like the pieces of a puzzle. If you look carefully, you will see a pair of bean-shaped cells called **guard cells**, which have a hole in the middle. This hole, called a **stoma** (plural, **stomata**), allows water and gases to enter and leave the leaf. When there is too much water, the guard cells swell up and open the stoma.

When the conditions are dry, the guard cells shrink and close the stoma, so that no additional water escapes. With the stain, it is easier to see the cell walls that make up the edges of the plant cells. The guard cells are also darker.

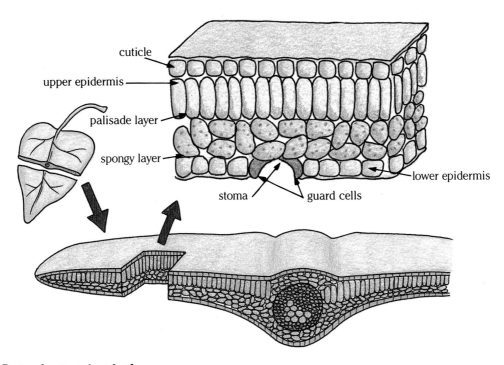

cuticle

upper epidermis

palisade layer

spongy layer

stoma    guard cells

lower epidermis

**Parts of a geranium leaf.**

# Water, Water Everywhere

*The oceans, lakes, ponds, and ditches of the world are filled with tiny living things. There are more small things living in a single drop of water than you may realize. Don't expect to find them swimming around in your drinking water, though. Most people drink water that has been purified and should not contain these small creatures. (If you do find them in your drinking water, tell your parents and the appropriate authorities!) Here is a simple way to collect samples and two different techniques for viewing them.*

**Note:** *The water you collect should not be stored near food. Containers and hands that have handled your water samples should be washed with soap and water. Clean up any spills with disinfectant. Do not eat when handling water samples or touch your eyes, nose, or mouth.*

## You Will Need

- large storage jar and lid
- thin piece of cloth, large enough to cover the top of the jar
- rubber band
- water from a pond, freshwater lake, or ditch
- uncooked rice
- adult helper

## What to Do

**1.** Take your large storage jar to the pond, lake, or ditch where you will collect your sample. Be sure to go with an adult helper.
**2.** Put some of the water you find into your jar. Add some of the leaves of plants growing at the edge of the water source.
**3.** Scoop some of the dirt from the bottom of the place where you sampled the water and add it to the jar.
**4.** Cover the jar with the lid. Be sure to wash your hands with soap and water after handling the water sample.
**5.** When you get home, remove the lid and add a few grains of rice to the jar. Cover the jar with a thin piece of cloth and use a rubber band to secure the cloth to the jar. Label the jar and store it in a cool, dark place until you are ready to look at the organisms. When you are finished with all the experiments, pour the water into your garden.

# MAKING AND USING A WELL SLIDE

Microscopists (people who use microscopes) sometimes use special slides called **well slides**. These slides have a small bowl-shaped hollow in the middle, which is useful for looking at specimens living in liquids such as pond water. If you have a well slide, you can use it to look at pond creatures; if not, here is a way to make a well slide.

## You Will Need

• slide and cover slip
• paper towel
• toothpick
• clear, colorless nail polish
• eyedropper

• pond water or water from a puddle or ditch
• microscope

## What to Do

**1.** Make a well slide following the directions in the box.
**2.** Using the eyedropper, carefully transfer a drop of your water sample to the center of the well.
**3.** Gently place the cover slip on top of the water drop. Do not press down. Blot up any water that spills out of the well with a paper towel.
**4.** Look at your slide using the low-power objective. You may have to reduce the amount of light going through the sample in order to see the aquatic creatures more easily. Move the slide around gently to see more of the organisms.
**5.** When you have found some of the organisms, place them in the center of your field of view and look at them with the high-power objective.

---

**MAKING A WELL SLIDE**

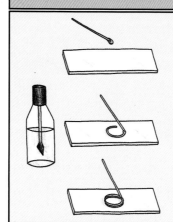

**A.** Place a slide on a clean paper towel on a flat surface.

**B.** In the center of the slide, use a toothpick to draw a circle about ½ inch (1 cm) in diameter with the nail polish. Allow the nail polish to dry.

**C.** Add several additional layers to the circle, allowing the nail polish to dry completely after applying each layer. This creates a well on the slide.

---

## What Happened

You probably saw tiny little creatures in the water. They may be rather strange-looking, and may even resemble something from an old science fiction movie! Some of the creatures are single-celled organisms, some are simple plants or simple animals. Try to identify them by looking at the accompanying diagrams, which show a few common freshwater creatures. If you see any others, draw pictures of them; then go to your local library and look them up in biology books. If you need to, ask the librarian for help.

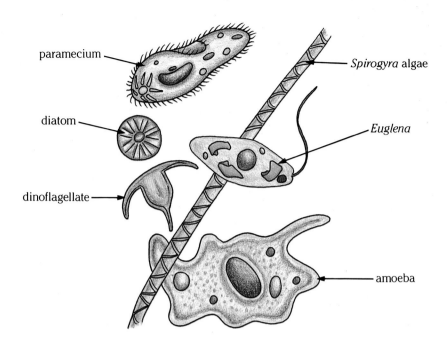

**Some common pond microorganisms.**

paramecium

*Spirogyra* algae

diatom

*Euglena*

dinoflagellate

amoeba

**5.** When you have found some organisms, move them to the center of your field of view and look at them with the high-power objective.

**Using cotton threads to slow down microorganisms.**

# COTTON THE ACT

Sometimes when you look at pond creatures under the microscope, they are difficult to see because they zip about through the water too quickly. You can slow them down by adding chemicals to the water, but that may kill them. Here is a gentler method of slowing them down.

## You Will Need

• cotton ball

• slide and cover slip

• eyedropper and pond water or other water sample

• microscope

## What to Do

**1.** Pull several strands from the cotton ball and place them in the center of the slide.

**2.** Use the eyedropper to transfer a drop or two of your water sample on top of the cotton strands.

**3.** Gently place the cover slip on top of the water and cotton strand. Do not press down.

**4.** Look at your slide using the low-power objective. You may have to reduce the amount of light going through the sample in order to see the water creatures more easily. Move the slide around gently to see more of the organisms.

## What Happened

The organisms in the water were slowed down by the cotton strands, which were in their way. The cotton strands also held up the cover slip, giving the organisms room to move.

# Along Came a Spider

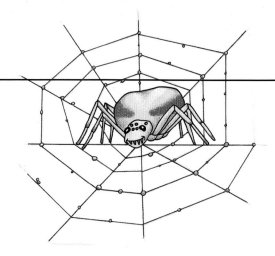

*See if you can find a spider web early in the morning when it is glistening with dew. You can see the water hanging in little droplets along the strands of the web. A spider web makes a wonderful slide, but you have to wait until it's dry so that it will stick to the slide. Using a microscope, you can begin to understand why insects cannot escape from the sticky web.*

## You Will Need

- clear, colorless nail polish
- slide and cover slip
- dry spider web
- stick
- microscope

## What to Do

**1.** Cover the center of a slide with a thin layer of clear, colorless nail polish. Allow the nail polish to set for about 1 minute.

**2.** Quickly place the slide on the center part of the web and pull the web towards you. Use a stick to knock away the outer edges of the web, so that they do not stick to you or the slide. Be sure not to knock the spider onto yourself when you do this.

**3.** Immediately cover the slide with the cover slip and press down gently.

**4.** Examine your slide under the microscope, using both the low-power and high-power objectives.

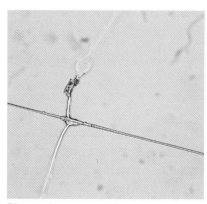

**Photomicrograph of spider web where two pieces join; photographed at 400× and enlarged.**

## What Happened

The type of spider web you collected probably was an orb web, formed by the common garden spider. It has rays that point outward, like the spokes of a wheel. The spider uses the sticky fibres of this web to catch small insects, which it eats. The strands of silk from the web have two parts: a long, elastic fibre and drops of gooey stuff. When the spider spins a web, it releases the web material from small pores on spinning organs called spinnerets, located between its back legs. The web material is made by silk glands inside the spider. Different shapes of spider webs are formed by other kinds of spiders.

# Sounds Fishy to Me

*When we think of a fish, we generally think of a scaly creature that lives in water. Just as a bird's feathers give it unique characteristics, a fish's scales have a distinctive pattern by which you can identify it. This experiment will show you some of the differences among fish scales, and you will also be able to tell whether a fish is old or young.*

## What You Need

- scales from different kinds of fish
- paper towelling
- water and small container
- eyedropper and tweezers
- slides and cover slips
- pen and paper
- microscope

## What to Do

**1.** Ask for samples of different fish scales at a supermarket, fish market, or another store that sells fresh seafood. Try to get scales that are pulled from the fish, rather than cut off.

**2.** Wrap each type of fish scale in wet paper towelling, and label each package, so that you can tell what kind of fish it came from. Place the wet towelling in a container to take home.

**3.** Unwrap each package of fish scales just before you wish to examine it. If your fish scales are really slimy, wipe off some of the moisture on a paper towel.

**4.** Make a wet mount of one scale from each of several kinds of fish, following the instructions on page 29, and label each slide.

**5.** Examine your slide under the microscope, using the low-power objective.

**6.** For each slide, write down the type of fish, the number of rings on the scale, the color of the scale, and the size of the scale in your journal.

**Photomicrograph of trout scale; photographed at 40× and enlarged.**

## What Happened

Scales are unique to each species of fish. If you look at a whole fish, you will notice that the scales overlap and attach to a fish in the same manner as the shingles do to the roof of a house. If you were constructing a fish, you would put the first layer of scales on at the tail and add each row partially overlapping the previous one, ending up with the last row at the fish's head. Some fish, like tuna, have interlocking scales. Over the years, tuna has evolved so that the scales now mesh together. Some fish, like salmon, have large, shiny scales. Sharks, on the other hand, don't have scales at all. Their skin has microscopic hooks that make it feel like rough sandpaper. Scientists are able to discover a fish's species by examining its scales. You also can tell something about the age of the fish by counting the rings on its scales. The older the fish is, the more rings there will be.

# Birds of a Feather

*Some birds have long colorful feathers; for example, peacocks. Some birds have big fluffy feathers; for example, ostriches or emus. Others, like geese or ducks, have thick, stiff feathers. Chicks and other baby birds have soft downy feathers. By examining some of these feathers under a microscope, you can begin to see the differences in the types of feathers.*

## You Will Need

- different kinds of feathers
- eyedropper and tweezers
- glycerine
- slides and cover slips
- scissors and tissue
- pen and paper
- microscope

## What to Do

**1.** Gather several different kinds of feathers. A good source of feathers might be your local zoo, pet store, or bird sanctuary. Ask the zookeeper or maintenance person to give you some of the feathers from the bird's cage or pen. Look around a park or even your yard for bird feathers. If you own a bird, gather feathers from the bottom of the cage. Some craft shops also sell individual feathers.

**2.** Use scissors to cut a small section from a feather, from the side of the shaft. You may wish to cut several sections from different parts of the feather.

**3.** Use the eyedropper to place 2 drops of glycerine on the center of the slide.

**4.** Place the feather sample on the glycerine, using the tweezers. Hold the cover slip upright so that one edge of the slip touches the edge of the drop of glycerine. Gently lower the cover slip over the glycerine and sample, trying not to trap any air bubbles. Blot up excess glycerine with a tissue or paper towel.

**5.** Record in your journal the type of feather and location of the section you cut, and label the slide.

**6.** Examine your slide under the microscope with both the low-power and high-power objectives.

**7.** Make several samples using different kinds of feathers. Be sure to wash all your equipment, as well as your hands, after handling the feathers, and throw away any leftover feathers.

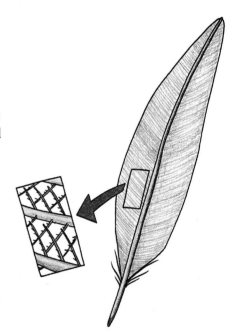

**Where to cut on a contour feather.**

a

b

**Photomicrographs of feathers: (a) contour of feather photographed at 40×; (b) down feather at 100×. Both enlarged.**

## What Happened

You saw dark lines that crossed the microscope slide. These lines are the parts of the feather. There are three main types of feathers: **contour feathers**, **down feathers**, and **filoplumes**. Contour feathers are the large exposed feathers that cover the bird's body. A contour feather has a central shaft and a tapering vane that grows out from the center shaft on either side, composed of barbs in parallel rows. Little hooks or barbicels hold the tiny strands of the feather to each other. Down feathers are soft, small feathers that grow underneath the contour feathers and keep the bird warm. They are simpler than contour feathers and don't have barbicels. Filoplumes are thin feathers with a single, hairlike shaft and a vane that is small or missing. The colorful tailfeathers of peacocks are filoplumes.

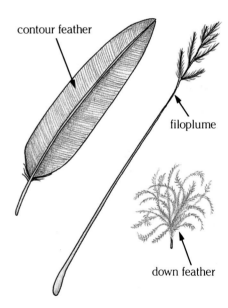

contour feather

filoplume

down feather

**The three types of feathers.**

# Don't Be Cheeky

*Now that you've studied parts of other living things, perhaps you're curious to see what some cells of your own body look like. Here is an easy, safe, and pain-less way of getting and examining some.*

## You Will Need

- wooden toothpick
- slide and cover slip
- water and eyedropper
- microscope
- tincture of iodine
- tissue paper or paper towel

## What to Do*

**1.** Use a new, clean wooden toothpick to *gently* scrape the in-side lining of your cheek.

**2.** With an eyedropper, place two drops of tincture of iodine on a clean glass slide. Stir the toothpick back and forth in the iodine to transfer the cheek cells. This will spread them out on the slide. *Do not put this toothpick back into your mouth.* Throw it away immediately.

**3.** Hold the cover slip upright so that one edge of the slip touches the edge of the drops of liquid. Gently lower the cover slip over the iodine and sample, trying not to trap any air bubbles.

**4.** Blot up any excess tincture of iodine with a tissue or paper towel.

**5.** Observe your slide under the microscope, using the low- and high-power objectives.

**6.** When you have finished view-ing the slide, wash it carefully using soap and water. Rinse it carefully to remove all of the cheek cells and iodine.

---

*\*Caution: Only gather cells from your own cheek, not anyone else's. Do not perform this experiment if you have a cold or the flu.*

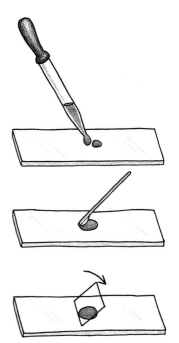

**Top: placing drops of iodine on a slide. Middle: stirring the cheek cells into the iodine. Bottom: lowering the cover slip.**

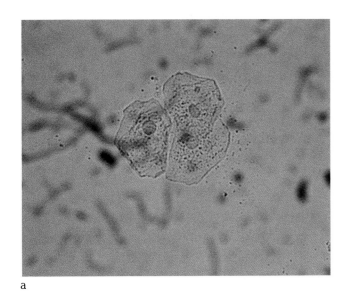
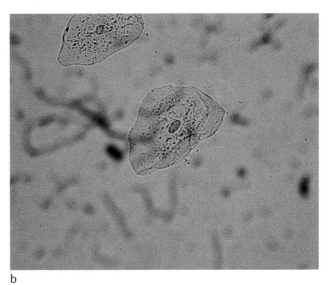

a
b

**Photomicrographs of cheek cells (a) without iodine; (b) with iodine. Both taken at 400× and enlarged.**

## What Happened

You saw small, irregularly shaped cheek cells. These cells do not look like plant cells because they do not have cell walls or chloroplasts. Instead, cheek cells, like all animal cells, have a thin covering called a **cell membrane**, which contains the cytoplasm. Plant cells also have cell membranes, but they are inside the cell walls, which means that they are hard to see. You also saw the nucleus, the small brown dot in the middle of the cell.

Your entire body is made up of cells. The cells in the lining of your cheek are constantly being replaced, so even though you removed some of them, new ones will grow in their place.

# *Tartar Control*

*Do your parents have to nag at you to brush your teeth? Maybe you'd be more encouraged to brush them if you knew that there were tiny fossils in your toothpaste. Here's an experiment to show you the prehistoric nature of your toothpaste; it will also help you discover one of the ways that toothpaste keeps your teeth clean.*

## You Will Need

- an abrasive toothpaste or tooth powder (a gel toothpaste will not work) or diatomaceous earth (from the hardware store)

- toothpick

- slides and cover slips

- microscope

- pen, paper, and cellophane tape

## What to Do

**1.** Use a toothpick to spread a tiny amount of toothpaste on the center of a slide.
**2.** Prepare a smear slide (see box).
**3.** Examine your slide under the microscope, using both the low-power and high-power objectives. What did you see?

**4.** Take a clean slide and squeeze a small amount of toothpaste on the center of the slide. Place another clean slide over the toothpaste and rub it back and forth over the first slide, so that the

slide is scratched. Rinse off the toothpaste and dry the slide. Try this technique with several different brands of toothpaste, labelling the slides with the brand used.

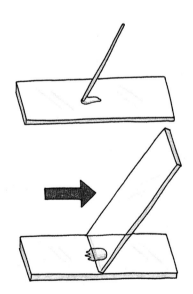

**Smear technique with toothpaste.**

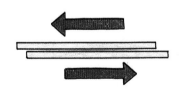

**Top: toothpaste placed between two slides. Bottom: slides with toothpaste between them being rubbed back and forth.**

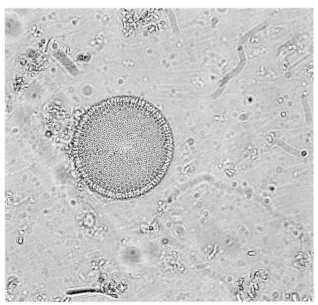

Photomicrograph of diatomaceous earth, taken at 400 × and enlarged.

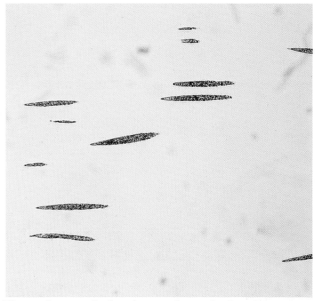

Photomicrograph showing toothpaste's abrasive action on slides, taken at 40 × and enlarged.

## What Happened

Some types of abrasive toothpaste contain microfossils that are the hardened remains of tiny one-celled aquatic plants called diatoms. Diatoms have shells made of silica, a compound used to make glass. When the diatoms died, they settled on the ocean floor or lake bottom, where they formed a hardened material called diatomaceous earth. This material may be used for polishing delicate objects, like silverware or your teeth. Brushing your teeth helps prevent tooth decay. The decay-causing plaque is removed from your teeth, but your teeth are not scratched. The glass slides were scratched very easily because the glass is not as hard as your teeth. If you rubbed two slides against each other with abrasive toothpaste in the middle, you may have scratched the slides. The more gentle the toothpaste, the less likely you are to see scratches on the glass slide. The scratches will look like thin, shiny lines going across the glass.

# Geology

**Y**ou may wonder what possible use a microscope could be in **geology**, the study of the earth. How could you possibly fit a rock sample on a tiny stage? Special microscopes called petrographic microscopes are used in the study of rocks and minerals. Petrographic microscopes have different kinds of lighting and very different kinds of stages than standard microscopes. **Metallurgy**, the science of extracting and separating ores and metals and finding uses for them, is a related field. Microscopes are extremely important in helping geologists and metallurgists tell how good a diamond is, or if a rock sample contains certain minerals or metals. When working with rocks, scientists sometimes use strong acids to wash away parts of the sample before they examine it under the microscope. They can also grind the sample down or use special equipment to thinly slice the sample before studying it. **Polarizing filters**, which allow the passage of light vibrating in one plane only, are used to help the scientists identify the sample. The polarized light makes the minerals shine with bright colors, which helps to identify them.

# Crystal Gazing

*Crystals are solids whose atoms are arranged in a repetitive order. Crystalline structures can make exciting and beautiful slides. You can make these slides easily from items commonly found in your kitchen. You can even use the tears left over from the Onion Rings experiment to create a truly personal slide.*

## You Will Need

- table salt and sugar
- borax*
- Epsom salts*
- tears
- alum* (available at most drugstores)
- slides
- stalk of rhubarb or fresh orange, lemon, or grapefruit juice
- teaspoon and water
- pen and paper
- microscope

---

*Do not taste or eat these.*

## What to Do

**1.** Fill a teaspoon halfway with very warm water. Add a few grains of table salt to the teaspoon and allow them to dissolve.

**2.** Move the slides to a windowsill where they can stay undisturbed for several days if necessary.

**3.** Gently pour the salt water onto a clean slide. Make sure you label the slide so you'll know what you are looking at. Do not move the slide until all the water has **evaporated** (changed from a liquid to a gas).

**4.** Make slides of sugar, borax, Epsom salts, and alum, following the same steps you used to make the table salt slide.

**5.** Squeeze some juice from the stem of a freshly cut rhubarb stalk onto the center of a slide. Allow the liquid to evaporate. (If you cannot find any rhubarb, try the juice from a fresh lemon, orange or grapefruit instead.)

**6.** Drop a tear onto a clean slide and allow it to dry. (You may have some left from your onion experiment.)

**7.** Observe all your slides under the microscope, using the low-power and high-power objectives. Compare the tear slide to the table salt slide. Do they look similar?

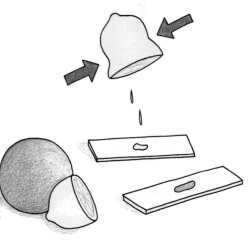

## What Happened

The salt crystals formed on the slide when the water evaporated. Table salt forms clear, colorless cube-shaped crystals. If you used iodized salt, you may have seen a few purple iodine crystals. The sugar sample was slower to form crystals. Epsom salts form arrow-shaped crystals. The different fruit samples are made up of several compounds, so you got a mixture of crystal shapes and sizes. One common crystal you may see in fruits is oxalic acid. Tears are a mixture of salt and other compounds, so they will produce several different shapes of crystals.

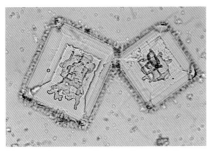

**Photomicrograph of salt crystals, taken at 400× and enlarged.**

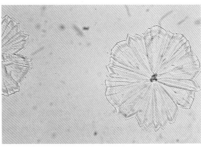

**Photomicrograph of sugar crystals, taken at 400× and enlarged.**

**Photomicrograph of borax crystals, taken at 100× and enlarged.**

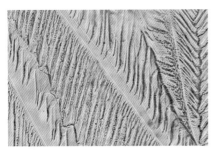

**Photomicrograph of Epsom salts crystals, taken at 100× and enlarged.**

**Photomicrograph of crystals of tears, taken at 400× and enlarged.**

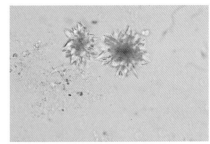

**Photomicrograph of rhubarb crystals, taken at 400× and enlarged.**

# Rock Hard

You probably think that rocks are too hard to cut into sections for your microscope. You certainly can't cut most rocks with a razor knife. Geologists study rock samples by cutting them into very thin slices with specialized equipment. Another way to look at the materials that make up rocks is to crush the rocks. Rocks are made up of minerals, and the same minerals are found crushed up as sand. You can easily look at these minerals with your microscope. Here's how.

## You Will Need

- slide
- pencil and labels
- sand from several locations
- microscope
- magnet and lamp

## What to Do

**1.** Label your slide with the location from which you got the sand sample. Place the slide on a flat surface near your microscope.

**2.** Sprinkle a few grains of sand onto the slide. Carefully transfer the slide to the stage of the microscope and secure it with the stage clips.

**3.** Use a lamp to light the sample from above.

**4.** Examine your slide under both the low-power and high-power objectives.

**5.** Prepare slides of the other sand samples. Observe any differences.

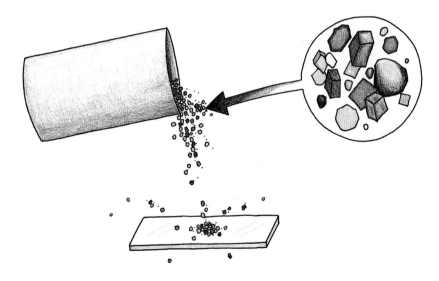

## What Happened

The sand grains look like crystals when viewed through the microscope. The sand samples are made of different minerals. Minerals occur in many colors, and each has a distinctive crystal shape. The most common mineral you will see is quartz. Quartz is usually white, but it can also be pinkish in color or even brownish, if small amounts of other compounds occur in the mineral. One other common mineral, magnetite, is black and can be picked up by a magnet. Try testing the black grains, if you find any in your sand samples, to see if you have magnetite. Another common mineral, calcite, is white and bubbles when mixed with acids. You may see some bubbling if you add a few drops of vinegar to a whitish sand sample. Sea salt forms a mineral called halite, which is also white and has small, cubic crystals. You may detect halite in some sands that you find near the ocean. There are many other minerals to be found in sand. To find out more about them, visit your local library and look for a book on rocks and minerals.

a

b

c

d

**Photomicrographs: Sand samples photographed (a) at 60×; (b) at 120×; (c) black sand at 120×; (d) sand with shells at 120×. All enlarged.**

# Take It for Granite

You probably think that you can only look at tiny things under a microscope. Well, usually, that's true. You can, however, if you are really careful, look at rocks. The trick is to find little rocks. You also must use extreme caution, so that you do not damage your objective by focusing too closely and hitting your sample. So empty those pockets of all those great stones you've been collecting and let's take a closer look at them.

## You Will Need

- samples of several smooth pebbles, about ¼″ × ¼″ (.6 cm × .6 cm)
- very fine-grained wet-or-dry sandpaper
- modelling clay
- eyedropper and water
- slides
- microscope
- lamp

## What to Do

**1.** Rub a rock sample in a circular motion over a piece of sandpaper. Frequently wet the rock with water, as this will make it easier to polish. Keep rubbing and wetting the rock until the surface of the rock is smooth.
**2.** Rinse the dust from the rock under running water.
**3.** Place a small blob of modelling clay in the center of a clean slide. Push the rock into the modelling clay so that the rock's smooth side faces upwards. Add a drop of water to the top of the rock.
**4.** Use a lamp to light the sample from above.
**5.** Observe your slide, using the low-power objective.

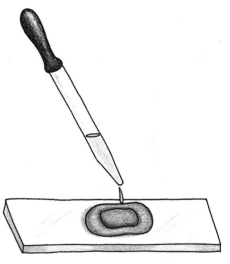

**Rock sample fixed onto slide with modelling clay.**

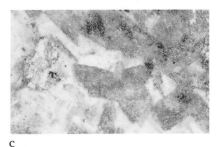

a          b          c

**Photomicrographs of rock samples taken (a) at 60×; (b) at 120×; (c) at 250×. All enlarged.**

## What Happened

When you looked at a smooth rock under a microscope, the surface may have looked quite rough. You may have seen the crystals of the minerals that make up the rock. The crystals in rock can be identified by their different colors and shapes. Some common minerals were described in the previous experiment. When geologists look at rock samples to learn which minerals they contain, they prepare thin slices of the rock. The rock is then polished and sometimes treated with acids or other chemicals. The samples are often viewed by using special lamps that have polarizing filters. The polarized light makes the minerals shine with bright colors, which geologists can use to identify the minerals.

If you have a pair of polarizing sunglasses, you can see how polarizing lenses work. Hold the glasses away from your face. Rotate the lenses while looking at the reflection from light from a puddle or pool of water. The amount of light coming through the lenses will change, depending on the angle at which you are holding the glasses.

# Forensic Science

**Forensic scientists** find microscopes very handy. Police use microscopes to study fingerprints, bits of clothing or fibres, hair, or other evidence that may have been left by criminals. Police laboratories even may be able to tell if a certain suspect committed a crime by examining the **DNA** from saliva, skin, blood, etc., found at the scene of a crime. Police laboratories have special microscopes that can compare the markings on bullets to see if they have been fired from the same gun. Credit cards and money can be examined to see if they are real. If a contract or a will is suspected of being a forgery (a false document), a microscope can help the experts decide if it is real.

Here's an easy experiment to tell if paper money is counterfeit (imitation) or real. Place the edge of a paper bill in the center of the microscope stage so an edge is over the hole, and use the stage clips to hold it in place. Focus the low-power objective on the edge of the bill. If the bill is real, you will be able to see tiny letters printed across the edge. Each country puts the tiny print in different places on its paper money. If there is no writing on the top of the bill, examine the bill in different places; there is something hidden on each bill to prove that it is real. Governments want to make sure that people do not photocopy money and try to use it. Photocopy machines cannot copy really small print on a bill; it will come out looking solid, so this is one way governments have to prevent counterfeiting.

# Give It a Whorl

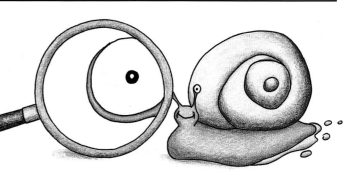

*Fingerprints are like snowflakes: each one is unique. No two people have the same fingerprints, not even twins. This makes it easy for police to determine if a fingerprint found at the scene of a crime belongs to the person they have arrested. Here are the three ways of making fingerprints and studying them.*

## You Will Need

- cotton ball
- fingernail polish remover containing acetone
- clear acetate or cellophane sheets
- slides
- scissors and tweezers
- inked stamp pad with washable ink
- magnifying glass
- soap and water
- talcum powder or corn starch
- clear cellophane tape
- notebook and pen
- microscope

## What to Do

METHOD 1: ACETATE PEEL

**1.** Make an acetate peel of your fingers, or a friend's fingers, following the directions in the box. Be sure to wash your hands well with soap and water after touching the nail polish remover.

**2.** Keep a record noting whose fingerprints you got, which fingers were sampled, and the age of the person.

**3.** Study the fingerprints and see what patterns you can recognize.

---

### ACETATE PEEL

**A.** Pour some nail polish remover containing acetone onto a cotton ball.

**B.** Wet the surface of the object from which you want to make a print with the cotton ball. Any item with a dry, rough, or textured surface will work well, but do not use this technique on any varnished, painted, or finished wood surfaces (it will remove the finish). Check with an adult before using this on any object.

**C.** Press the wet surface of the object into the acetate or cellophane sheet.

**D.** Leave the object on the acetate sheet for several minutes to allow the print to set.

**E.** Carefully peel off or pull the sheet away from the object. Clean the object well with soap and water.

**F.** Hold the acetate peel with tweezers and use scissors to cut a sample to fit on the center of a slide, and place it on the slide.

**G.** Examine your slide under the low-power objective.

---

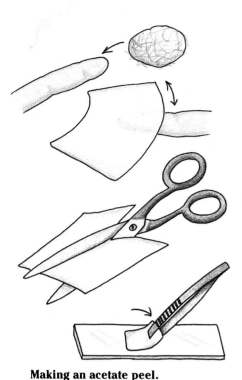

**Making an acetate peel.**

objective. What patterns can you see now? Keep a record as you did in Method 1.

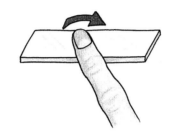

**Stamp-pad method.**

with the side of your finger over the tape in order to transfer the print.
**5.** Lift the tape and place it sticky side down in the center of a slide.
**6.** Examine your slide under the microscope, using the low-power objective. See if you can figure out to whom the print belongs.

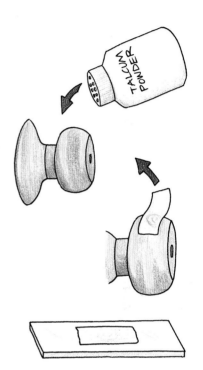

**Talcum powder method.**

## METHOD 2: STAMP PAD

**1.** Press a finger into the inked stamp pad. Make sure the finger-print part of the finger is completely covered with ink, including the sides.
**2.** Roll the inked finger from side to side on a clean slide. Do not lift the finger while rolling it, or your print will be fuzzy.
**3.** Lift the finger and immediately wash the inky hands with soap and water. This will keep the surfaces of the table, microscope, and especially the walls of your house, clean.
**4.** View the slide, using a magnifying glass. See what patterns you can recognize.
**5.** Examine your slide under the microscope, using the low-power

## METHOD 3: TALCUM POWDER

**1.** Look around your house for fingerprints. If you have a younger brother or sister, fingerprints are probably all over everything. Smooth surfaces like polished tables, doorknobs, and mirrors are good places to look. *Ask an adult's permission before performing the next step.*
**2.** Sprinkle a small amount of talcum powder or corn starch on a fingerprint. Blow away the loose powder. The fingerprint should be clearly visible.
**3.** Tear off a piece of cellophane tape slightly larger than the fingerprint.
**4.** Holding one end of the tape, press the rest of the tape over the fingerprint. Rub back and forth

## What Happened

In each of the methods above, you made a clear fingerprint. The acetone in the first method reacted with the chemicals in the acetate or cellophane sheet and dissolved the sheet in places, leaving the fingerprint. In the second method, the ink covered the ridges (the parts of the fingerprint that are raised), while leaving the furrows (the deeper parts of the fingerprint) without much ink. When the inked finger was rolled on the slide, the ridges, which were more heavily inked, left a print. In the third method, oil or dirt on a person's hands acted like ink and left a print. The talcum powder stuck to the print. The cellophane tape lifted the talcum powder and transferred the print to the slide.

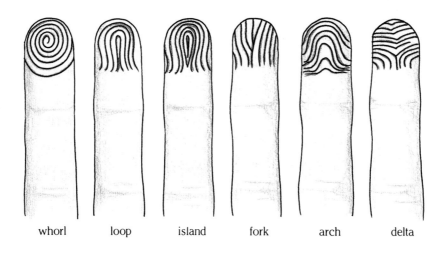

whorl    loop    island    fork    arch    delta

**Some of the features of fingerprints that experts use to help identify them: arch, loop, whorl, delta, island, fork.**

# Hair's Looking at You, Kid!

*In addition to fingerprints, police scientists study other materials found at the scenes of crimes. Fibres of hairs found at the scene can be important clues to help catch a criminal. Fibres can be matched to carpets or clothing. Samples of hair can be matched to see if the hair was bleached or dyed, and what part of the body it came from. You can be a detective, too. You can even tell if a hair is from an animal or a person. So clean up some old hairbrushes and let's get started!*

## You Will Need

- hair from several family members, friends, or pets
- plastic sandwich bag for each sample
- slides and cover slips
- water and eyedropper
- pen and paper or labels
- tweezers
- tissue paper or paper towel
- microscope

## What to Do

**1.** Collect hair samples from family members, friends, or pets, and put each in a bag along with a small paper saying whose hair it is. You can either pluck the hairs out (if people give you permission), or brush the person's or pet's hair and remove the hairs from the brush.

**2.** Cut a sample for each kind of hair about ¼″ long (0.6 cm) and make a wet mount of each hair sample, following the steps on page 29. Label each slide with its source.

**3.** Examine the first slide under the microscope, using the low-power and high-power objectives.

**4.** Take the other hair samples and examine them in the same way. You may wish to draw pictures of the different samples in your journal.

**Wet-mount technique with hair.**

## What Happened

You saw the three parts of each piece of hair. Hair is made up of tough, fibrous proteins called keratins. The outer, scaly layer is called the cuticle. You may need to change the focus slightly to see the cuticle clearly. Inside the cuticle is a tubular layer of keratin that gives hair strength, called the cortex. Inside the cortex is the medulla, a spongy inner core that contains grains of **pigment**, or colored material. In older people, less pigment is produced, and so the hair appears to be white. In general, brown hair tends to be thicker than blond hair, and blond hair tends to be thicker than red hair. Dyed hair may be coated on the outside of the shafts or permanently colored inside the hair shafts. If you are studying dyed hair, you may be able to get an undyed or unbleached sample of hair near the hair root, to which the dyed section can be compared. The sizes of the three hair layers (cuticle, cortex, and medulla) are quite different in animals than they are in people. In animals, the medulla is usually thicker compared to the cortex. The hair of some animals (for example, sheep) may have no medulla at all.

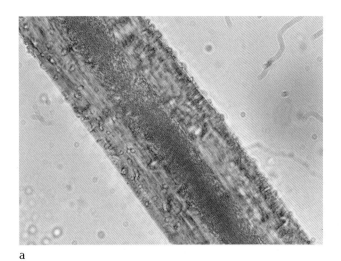

a

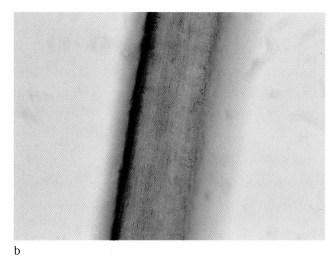

b

**Photomicrographs of hair made under high power (400×) and enlarged: (a) undyed blond hair; (b) dyed brown hair.**

# Fibre Optics

*Have you ever noticed that some clothing feels really soft, but other clothing feels rough and itchy? Do you love the feel of your favorite sweater or the smoothness of a satin jacket? By looking at different fabrics under a microscope, you can begin to discover what makes their fibres unique.*

## You Will Need

- a piece of cloth, clothing, or thread made from each of the following (or as many as you can get): silk, wool, nylon, polyester, linen, cotton, and mixed blends (for example, 50% cotton/50% polyester)
- scissors
- slides and cover slips
- eyedropper and water
- microscope
- pen and paper or labels

## What to Do

**1.** You do not have to cut up a piece of clothing or cloth to obtain your sample. Turn a garment inside out and look along the seams for any loose fibres. Ask a parent to help you cut off a loose fibre about ½ inch (1 cm) long.

**2.** Make a wet mount of the fibre, following the instructions on page 29. Label the slide so that you know where it came from and what it is made of.

**3.** Observe your slide under the microscope, using the low-power and high-power objectives. Keep a record of what the materials look like in your journal.

**4.** Repeat steps 2 and 3 for each kind of fibre you want to sample. Using your knowledge of fibres, see if you can tell what fibres make up your "mixed blends" sample.

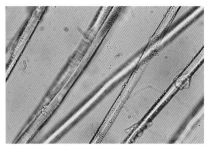

**Photomicrograph of silk; taken at 400 × and enlarged.**

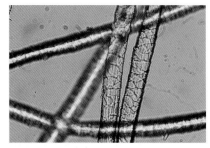

**Photomicrograph of wool; taken at 400 × and enlarged.**

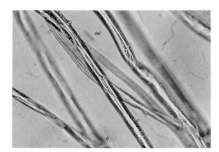

**Photomicrograph of cotton; taken at 400 × and enlarged.**

**Photomicrograph of nylon; taken at 400 × and enlarged.**

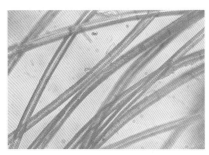

**Photomicrograph of polyester; taken at 400 × and enlarged.**

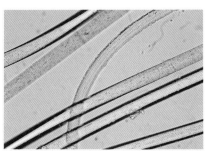

**Photomicrograph of linen; taken at 400 × and enlarged.**

## What Happened

Each fibre has its own distinct appearance. Wool looks broken or scaly, because of the keratin plates on the hair (wool is sheep's hair). Threads made from plant fibres, such as cotton or linen, resemble each other. Cotton looks like a flattened tube or ribbon, while linen looks like a more rounded, thicker version of cotton. Silk is made from thread spun by a silkworm. Silk fibre looks like a piece of glass; it is round, even, and solid. Threads of synthetic fabrics, such as nylon and polyester, are chemically produced; their shape can vary, depending on how they are spun. Some polyester fibres are lumpy. As these lumps gather, they form "pills." If you have an old polyester garment, you may see pills on the surface of the material.

# Food & the Environment

Scientists who study the environment use microscopes to help them determine how polluted water is; what damage has been done to the soil; and even what kinds of pollutants are found in the air, land, and the food you eat. Using this information, scientists can find out if pollution is harming or killing the living creatures in a certain area. Without microscopes, scientists would not be able to measure the damage being done to the environment. Before the invention of microscopes, some foods (for example, milk) were unsafe to eat or drink. Now scientists can look at food samples and monitor the microscopic organisms that cause food to rot and spoil.

# One Potato, Two Potato

*Many of the foods we eat contain **starch**. Corn has starch, so do potatoes, peas, rice, sweet potatoes, oats, and other grains. When viewed under a microscope, starch grains have varied shapes, depending on the source of the starch. Here is a way of comparing the shapes of grains of different starches and seeing the effect of iodine and saliva on these samples, using your microscope.*

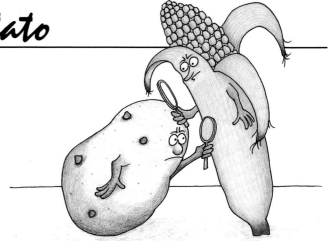

## You Will Need

- small piece of white potato and sweet potato
- knife and spoon
- cooked rice, peas, corn or other starchy vegetable
- slides and cover slips
- well slide
- paper towelling
- tincture of iodine
- eyedropper and water
- microscope
- pen and paper

## What to Do

**1.** Use the knife to lightly scrape a bit of potato from the freshly cut surface of the white potato.

**2.** Place this scraping in the center of a clean slide and make a wet mount of the slide (see instructions on page 29).

**3.** Observe your slide under the microscope, using the low- and high-power objectives.

**4.** Place the slide on some paper towelling on a table.

**5.** Stain the slide with tincture of iodine, following the instructions on page 31 for pulling a stain.

**6.** View this slide under the microscope again, as in step 3. What differences do you notice? Set the slide aside.

**7.** Scrape another fresh sample of white potato starch into a well slide. (See directions on page 40 for making a well slide, if necessary.)

**8.** Place a clean spoon in your mouth and gather a small amount of saliva in the spoon.

**9.** Transfer the saliva into the hollow in the well slide and place a cover slip on top of the well. Leave the slide in a warm place.

**10.** Every 10 minutes, observe the slide under the low- and high-

power objectives. Record the changes you see during the next hour in your journal.

**11.** Repeat the above experiment, using different sources of starch, including sweet potato, rice, peas, and corn. How do the samples of starch differ from the potato starch?

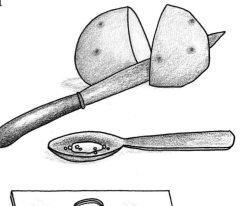

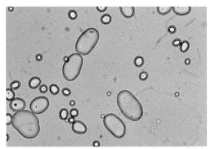

**Photomicrograph of potato starch, taken at 400× and enlarged.**

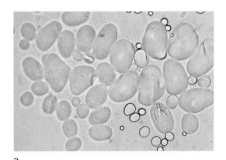

a

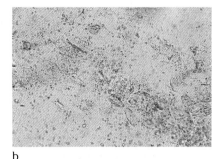

b

**Photomicrograph of potato starch, iodine, and saliva: (a) after 5 minutes; (b) after 15 minutes; both taken at 400×, and enlarged.**

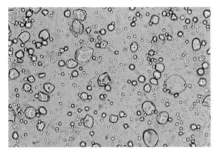

**Photomicrograph of sweet potato starch and iodine; taken at 400× and enlarged.**

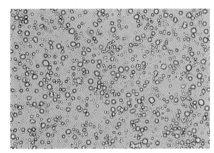

**Photomicrograph of corn starch and iodine; taken at 400× and enlarged.**

## What Happened

You saw large, distinct grains of starch in your samples. The iodine reacted with the starch and changed from brownish red to a bluish black color. The starch grains appear to be bluish black because of the iodine. Potato starch has large grains, which show irregular oval rings that fit inside each other. Starch is an organic chemical that plants make to store sugar. It is made up of sugar molecules joined together. When the potato starch was mixed with saliva, something interesting happened. The saliva broke apart the links between the sugar molecules and changed the starch back into sugar. The sugar dissolved in the saliva, making the grains disappear. The other types of starch looked quite different under the microscope. For example, corn starch has smaller, many-sided grains.

# They Broke the Mould*

When a food has become mouldy, it usually means that it is not good to eat. Moulds are one type of **fungi**. Fungi have no chlorophyll, so they can't make their own food. They have to grow on other living or dead plants or animals. Yeasts and mushrooms also are fungi. Although moulds may all look the same to you, there are many different kinds. Blue moulds are found on certain types of cheese and on citrus fruits. Grey mould is usually found on berries. Rhizopus (black bread mould) is usually associated with breads and baked goods; black mould or smut is found on vegetables such as onions. Meats sometimes get green mould. And, of course, there's mildew, a kind of mould usually associated with shower walls and gym lockers! So ask your parents not to throw away that green bread. It's really a science experiment!

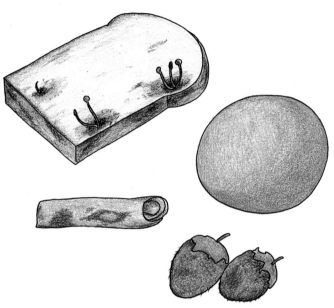

## You Will Need

- mould from some or all of the following: bread, oranges and lemons, blue cheese, strawberries or other fruit, and onions
- toothpick or needle
- water and eyedropper
- slides and cover slips
- microscope
- pencil, pen and labels

*Warning: if you are allergic to mould, do not perform this experiment. Do not experiment with mouldy meat.

## What to Do

**1.** Look around your kitchen to see if you can find any food that has become mouldy. If there isn't any, sprinkle a cut-up orange, a strawberry, or a cut-up onion with water, and put it on the counter for about a week and it probably will grow some. You can also grow mould by sprinkling a few drops of water on a slice of bread and sealing it in a plastic bag for a few days. Your grocer may be willing to let you have some small samples of mouldy fruit, vegetables, or cheese.

**2.** Use a toothpick or a needle to scrape a small bit of mould from each food. Do this carefully so that you do not damage the sample.
**3.** Place the mould from each on its own slide and make a wet mount, following the instructions on page 29. Label each slide with its source.
**4.** Observe your slides under the microscope, using the low- and high-power objectives. Record your observations.
**5.** When you are finished, wash your equipment and hands well with soap and water.

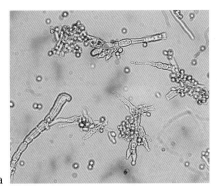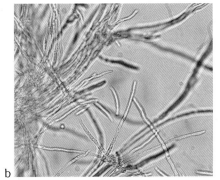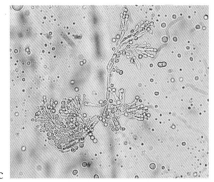

a                                   b                                c

**Photomicrographs of moulds: (a) on orange; (b) on papaya; (c) on cheddar cheese; all taken at 400× and enlarged.**

## What Happened

You saw that the fuzzy material that makes up the mould is really small threadlike filaments. These filaments are called **hyphae**. They are matted together in a mesh, called a **mycelium**, that spreads out over the food sample. The hyphae not only hold the moulds in place, but also take in nutrients. This explains why moulds seem to eat away at the food on which they grow. You may have seen small dots or thicker sections on the ends of the hyphae. These dots are called **fruiting bodies** and they contain **spores**. Using the high-power objective, you may see some spores that are very tiny. These single-celled particles can be long and thin or almost spherical. In many ways spores are similar to seeds. They are released from the fruiting bodies and grow to produce new moulds.

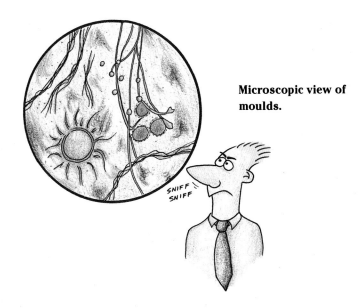

**Microscopic view of moulds.**

# The Blob

*Have you ever watched anyone make bread? What starts out as a small amount of flour and yeast soon grows into a huge, sweet-smelling bowl of sticky dough. This dough is then punched down, only to rise again. Yeast is used in baking bread because it gives off carbon dioxide as it grows, which makes bubbles in the bread dough and causes the dough to puff up or rise. Yeast also gives off ethanol as it grows. Ethanol is the type of alcohol in beer, wine, and liquor. Here is an experiment to examine the way yeast grows.*

## You Will Need

- teaspoon (5 mL) of yeast
- sugar or corn syrup
- 1 cup (240 mL) warm water and bowl
- eyedropper and teaspoon
- cloth to cover bowl
- slides and cover slips
- pen and paper
- microscope
- tincture of iodine

## What to Do

**1.** Place a teaspoon (5 mL) of yeast in a bowl. Add 1 cup (240 mL) of lukewarm water to the bowl. Do not use *hot* water, as this will kill the yeast.

**2.** Add about a teaspoon (5 mL) of sugar or corn syrup to the warm water and yeast, and mix the solution.

**3.** Use an eyedropper to place a small drop of the yeasty liquid on a clean slide.

**4.** Gently lower the cover slip over the drop of liquid, trying not to trap any air bubbles.

**5.** Observe your slide under the microscope, using the low- and high-power objectives. Record what you see.

**6.** Cover the bowl of yeasty liquid with a cloth and place it in a warm spot overnight.

**7.** The next day, dilute a few drops of the tincture of iodine with an equal number of drops of tapwater, so that it is not as strong.

**8.** Use the eyedropper to place a drop of the yeast solution on a clean slide.

**9.** Stain the slide with the diluted iodine mixture and cover it with the cover slip.

**10.** View the slide as in step 5 above. Does it look any different from the one you viewed yesterday?

**11.** When you are finished, wash your slides, cover slips, all your materials, and your hands with soap and water.

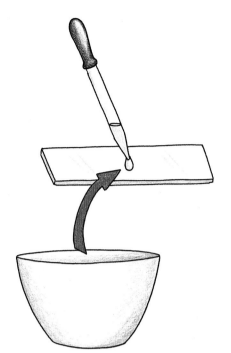

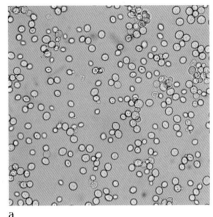

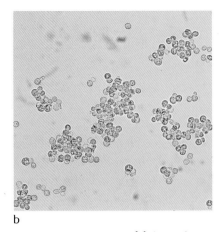

a

b

**Photomicrographs of yeast cells, taken at 400 × and enlarged: (a) just after adding to water without iodine; (b) several hours after adding to water with iodine.**

## What Happened

Yeast, another fungus, is made up of small egg-shaped single cells. The yeast used the sugar or corn syrup as food and grew. When a yeast cell gets too large, it becomes longer and forms a bud. When the bud is large enough, it separates to form a new yeast cell.

The iodine made the yeast cells easier to see. The cell's **nucleus** was stained darker by the iodine and any starch grains became bluish black.

# I'm Spored

**Question:** *Where do frogs sit?*
**Answer:** *On toad stools.*

**Question:** *What did one girl mushroom say to the other girl mushroom?*
**Answer:** *That boy mushroom over there looks like a real fungi (fun guy).*

*Yes, this experiment will examine mushrooms. Now that you've had a chance to look at various other kinds of fungi, such as moulds and yeasts, here's an easy way to take a closer look at spores. You'll find that the spores produced by different types of mushrooms make weird viewing.\**

## You Will Need

- several varieties of fresh mushrooms
- slides and cover slips
- clear plastic containers or glass jars
- water and eyedropper
- microscope
- pencil and labels

---

*\*Warning: Do not taste or eat any mushrooms that you have gathered from the garden or forest; they may be poisonous. Wash your hands and equipment with soap and water after this experiment and be sure to throw away any unknown mushrooms so they aren't mistaken for food, when you're done.*

## What to Do

**1.** Collect several different types of mushrooms: white-and-brown mushrooms from the grocery store, shiitake (Japanese mushrooms), morels, and any other kind of nonpoisonous mushrooms. Break off the stem of the mushroom so that it will sit flat on top of a slide.
**2.** Place the mushroom on a slide and label the slide.
**3.** Place a jar or container over the slide and mushroom and leave it in a warm place for about two days. The mushroom will release spores.
**4.** Remove the jar or container from the top of the slide. Make a wet mount of the spores following the instructions on page 29.

**5.** Observe your wet-mount slide under the microscope, using the low-power and high-power objectives.

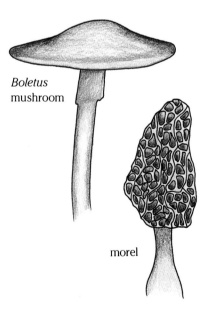

*Boletus* mushroom

morel

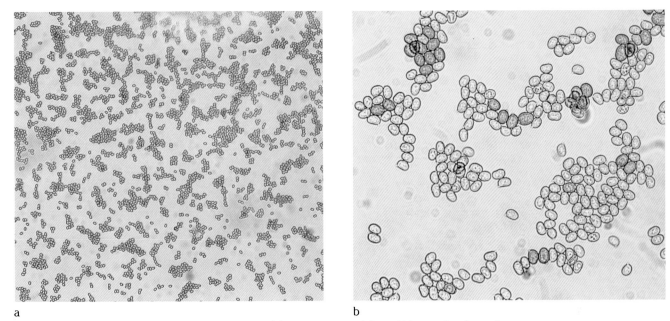

a

b

**Photomicrograph of mushroom spores, taken (a) at 100× and (b) at 400× and enlarged.**

## What Happened

The mushroom ripened in the warm jar and released its spores. Each type of mushroom had a different-shape spore. Outdoors, the mushroom releases its spores into the wind. If they land in a place where conditions are right, they will germinate and grow a new fungus, which will produce a new mushroom. The mycelium of the mushroom is underground.

The mushrooms are the fruiting bodies of the fungus. The mycelium grows to form a circle and the mushrooms sprout at the outside edges, where there is the most food. This is why mushrooms tend to grow in rings.

# Blowing in the Wind

*Fresh air is a wonderful thing. Most people think that if they are breathing fresh air, they are breathing air with nothing added. This isn't necessarily true. Even in the countryside, there are microscopic things in the air. Here is a way to sample the quality of the air around you and to see some of the things in the air you breathe.*

## You Will Need

- thin wire coat hanger
- cellophane tape
- cover slip and slide
- scissors
- lens paper
- microscope

## What to Do

**1.** Bend the coat hanger so the triangular part forms a square that has the hook of the hanger in the middle of one side, which will be the top.

**2.** Attach 5 or 6 long pieces of cellophane tape to the hanger so they stretch across the square opening from the top to the bottom of the hanger. This is your sampler.

**3.** Hang your sampler outside to test the air. Leave it undisturbed overnight.

**4.** The next day, take down the sampler and bring it inside. Press a clean cover slip carefully onto the cellophane tape part of the sampler. Choose an area of tape that looks at though it may have particles from the air on it. Carefully trim off the tape that extends beyond the edges of the cover slip. Place the cover slip on the slide so that the cover slip is on top and the tape is in the middle between the cover slip and the slide.

**5.** Examine your slide under the microscope, using both the low-power and high-power objectives.

**6.** Make a second slide of a clean, unused piece of cellophane tape and compare it to the one of the tape exposed to the outside air.

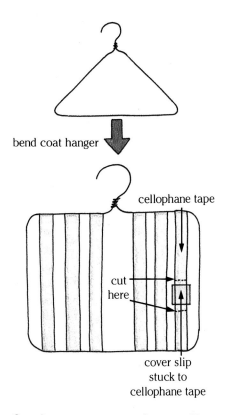

bend coat hanger

cellophane tape

cut here

cover slip stuck to cellophane tape

**Coat hanger apparatus for sampling air quality.**

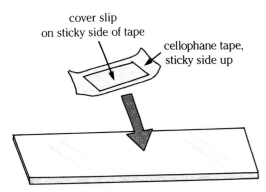

cover slip
on sticky side of tape

cellophane tape,
sticky side up

**The cover slip plus tape is placed on the slide for viewing.**

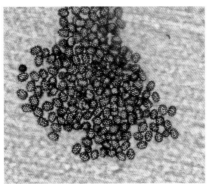

a

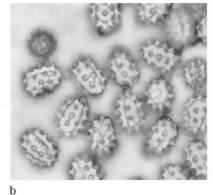

b

**Photomicrographs showing tape with pollen and dust, taken (a) at 100×; (b) at 400×. Both enlarged.**

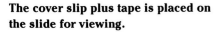

## What Happened

What people find on their slides varies. In some areas people will find pollen grains. In other places the air may carry small sand grains or dust particles (see Rock Hard for more about sand). Tiny bits of plants and hairs are also common. Air that carries a great deal of pollen can cause problems for people with allergies. Blackish dust in your sample may be air pollution.

# The Yolk's on You

*By now you've worked your way through all the scientific experiments in this book and you are probably ready for something that is just plain fun. Here's a way to create some beautiful, colorful closeups. If you have a camera attachment for your microscope, you may want to take some pictures of these slides. They will make great prints for mounting on your walls and perfect gifts for parents and teachers.*

## You Will Need

- a raw egg
- two containers and a saucer
- slides
- eyedropper or paintbrush
- several colors of food coloring and a paper towel
- water
- microscope
- camera attachment and film (optional)

## What to Do

**1.** Separate the egg yolk from the white. Place the egg white in a container. Throw away the egg yolk, or save it for baking.

**2.** Use a paintbrush or your finger to cover one side of the slide with some of the egg white.

**3.** Mix the food coloring to create whatever colors you like on the saucer. If a color is too dark, you can add a small amount of water to dilute it.

**4.** Use the eyedropper or paintbrush to place drops of food coloring on the top of the egg-white-coated surface of the slide. Allow the slide to dry.

**5.** Observe your slide under the microscope, using the low-power and high-power objectives.

**6.** If you have a camera attachment for your microscope, take pictures of your favorite slides.

**7.** Be sure to wash your hands and any equipment that touched the raw egg with hot, soapy water. (Raw eggs sometimes carry harmful bacteria.)

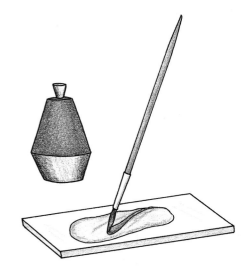

## What Happened

You created a beautiful slide! The food coloring dyed the egg white in an interesting way. The colors are shiny because of the protein in the egg white.

**Photomicrographs of raw egg with food coloring, taken at 40 × and enlarged.**

# GLOSSARY

**acetate peel:** a printmaking technique used to study the surface features of objects

**arm:** the curved part of the microscope that holds the body tube in place over the stage and base

**atom:** the smallest particle of an element, which cannot be divided further by chemical means

**base:** the heavy bottom part of the microscope

**biotechnology:** an applied biological science that changes the characteristics of living things to serve a technological purpose

**body tube:** the tube-shaped part of the microscope stand that holds the nosepiece and objectives on one end and the eyepiece on the other

**cell:** the smallest unit of an organism capable of functioning on its own

**cell membrane:** the thin covering surrounding the cell

**cell wall:** the limiting layer of material surrounding plant cells

**chlorophyll:** a green pigment contained in chloroplasts that allows plants to use the sun's energy to produce food

**chloroplasts:** small green structures containing chlorophyll in plant cells

**chromatic aberration:** defect of a lens that causes a rainbow effect when light is dispersed through the lens

**chromosomes:** threadlike structures in the nucleus of the cell that contain the hereditary information needed to make new cells

**coarse adjustment knob:** the large knob on the side of the microscope that quickly adjusts the distance between the object and the objective (and thus, the focus)

**compound lens:** a lens made of two or more lenses glued or stuck together

**compound microscope:** a microscope that magnifies in two stages by means of an objective and an eyepiece

**concave lens:** a lens that is thinner in the middle than it is at the edges

**condenser:** a part of the lighting system of the microscope that collects, controls, and concentrates light

**contour feathers:** the large feathers on a bird that give the body its shape

**convex lens:** a lens that is thicker in the middle and thinner on the edges

**cortex:** (1) the long hollow tubelike part of a hair strand that gives it strength. (2) The layer in a plant root and stem between the epidermis and xylem and phloem

**cover slip (cover glass):** a thin piece of glass or plastic that is placed on top of the sample on a slide

**crystal:** a solid whose atoms are arranged in a repetitive order

**cytoplasm:** the fluid inside a cell, surrounding the nucleus

**cytoplasmic streaming:** the movement of cytoplasm in a cell

**depth of field:** distance from the objective through which an object may be moved and still remain in focus

**diameter:** the widest distance across the field of view (or across any circle)

**diaphragm:** the part of the microscope that restricts the area of the light path shining through the sample

**DNA:** deoxyribonucleic acid; the compound contained in the nucleus of a cell that carries genetic information and controls functions

**down feathers:** the soft under-feathers of a bird

**electron microscope:** a microscope that uses a stream of electrons to form magnified images of samples

**epidermis:** the outermost layer of cells of a plant or animal

**eyepiece (ocular):** the lens system in a microscope that is nearest your eye; it magnifies the image formed by the objective

**evaporate:** to change from a liquid into gas

**fibre (fiber):** a thread, or structure or object that looks like a thread

**field of view:** the area of a slide that you can see through the eyepiece

**fine adjustment knob:** the small knob on the side of the microscope that lets you make small adjustments to the focus

**fruiting bodies:** structures containing spores, found at the ends of hyphae

**fungi:** plantlike organisms that lack chlorophyll and get their nutrition from other living or dead plants or animals. Fungi include moulds, yeasts, and mushrooms.

**geology:** the study of the earth

**graticule:** a scale or grid used for measuring the size of objects seen through the microscope

**guard cells:** pairs of bean-shaped cells surrounding the stoma on the epidermis of plants

**hyphae** (singular, **hypha**): threadlike filaments that make up the mycelium of a fungus

**index of refraction:** the ratio of the speed of light in a vacuum to its speed in a particular substance.

**litre (liter):** unit of liquid volume in the metric system, equal to 1.06 quarts

**lenticels:** pores containing pockets of air, found in the stems of woody plants

**magnification:** the amount that the dimensions of an image are or appear to be enlarged compared to the same dimensions in the object

**microbiology:** the study of microorganisms and their effect on other organisms and the environment

**micrometer eyepiece:** an eyepiece equipped with a scale for measuring samples

**micrometre (micrometer):** 1/1 000 000 metre; abbreviated μm

**microscopists:** people who are specialists in using microscopes

**microtome:** a machine for cutting thin slices of a sample

**millilitre (milliliter):** metric unit of liquid volume that is 1/1000 of a litre; abbreviated mL.

**millimetre (millimeter):** metric unit of length that is 1/1000 metre; abbreviated mm.

**mineral:** a solid, crystalline naturally occurring chemical element or compound

**mould (mold):** a fungus that produces a fluffy growth on food or other material

**mycelium:** the mat of hyphae that makes up most of the growing part of a fungus

**nucleus:** the spherical body in a cell that contains the chromosomes

**object:** the thing you want to study with a microscope or lens

**objective:** the part of the microscope's imaging system closest to the sample

**ocular:** *See* eyepiece

**oil immersion lens:** a special type of lens that is used by placing a drop of oil between the lens and the cover slip

**optical density:** the property of a medium that determines the speed of light in that medium

**optics:** the science that studies light and optical instruments

**organism:** an individual that can carry out the activities of life

**palisade cells:** oblong cells in leaves that make food for the plant

**phloem:** the food-conducting vascular tissues in plants

**photosynthesis:** the process by which green

plants create food from carbon dioxide and water using sunlight for energy

**pigment:** a substance that gives color to a thing, plant, or animal

**polarizing filter:** a filter that allows light to travel through it in one plane only

**pollen:** microspores that contain the male cells released from the anthers of flowering plants

**power:** the amount of magnification of a lens or lens system, abbreviated ×

**pulling a stain:** a technique for applying stain to a sample without removing the cover slip

**pupil:** small opening in the iris of the eye through which light enters

**real image:** a magnified image that can be projected onto a surface; compared to the object it is upside down

**refraction:** the bending of light that occurs at the boundary between one medium and another when light strikes it at an angle

**refractive index:** *See* index of refraction

**resolving power:** the ability of a lens to allow you to see fine detail

**retina:** light-sensitive layer at the back of the eye

**revolving nosepiece:** the part of the microscope that holds the objectives, which can be rotated into place

**sample:** the object or part of an object you wish to study or observe

**slide:** a thin, rectangular piece of glass on which a microscope sample is placed

**spores:** single-celled seedlike structures found in fungi

**stage:** the flat surface of the microscope on which you put your slide

**stage clips:** metal clips that hold the slide in place on the microscope stage

**stage micrometer:** glass slide with a built-in scale (reticule) for measuring specimens

**stain:** 1. (verb): to color an object; 2. (noun):

the material used to color the object

**starch:** a grainy white organic chemical that is the main storage for food in plants

**stoma** (plural, **stomata**): a hole in the epidermis of the underside of a leaf, which is surrounded by guard cells, that allows water and gases to enter and to leave the leaf

**vacuoles:** storage sacs for food, waste, or water found in many cells

**vascular bundles:** bundles of xylem and phloem cells packed together in a plant

**virtual image:** a magnified image that is right-side up and that cannot be projected onto a surface

**well slide:** a slide with a hollow in the center

**wet mount:** temporary way of preparing a microscope sample in a liquid medium between the slide and cover slip

**xylem:** water- and mineral-transporting tubelike plant tissues; they also provide support

# INDEX